Networking Basics

Project Manual

FRANK MILLER

PROJECT EDITOR	Brian B. Baker
MARKETING MANAGER	Jennifer Slomack
PRODUCTION MANAGER	Kelly Tavares
PRODUCTION EDITOR	Kerry Weinstein

To order books or for customer service please call 1-800-CALL WILEY (225-5945).

ISBN   978-0-470-12799-5

Printed in the United States of America

10 9 8 7 6 5 4 3 2

PREFACE

Networking Basics Project Manual is a learning tool for individuals who are new to networking, as well as those who seek to expand their skills in the field. It is an ideal companion to Ciccarelli et al.'s *Networking Basics* (Copyright 2008, John Wiley & Sons, 978-0-470-11129-1).

Easy-to-read, practical, and up-to-date, this Project Manual includes activities that reinforce the fundamentals of networking concepts while helping students develop core competencies and real-world skills. The sheer variety and span of activities let students learn at their own pace.

Each chapter contains five to seven projects. Projects range from easy to more advanced, and many include multiple parts. Each project contains the following elements:

- Overview: Introduces the topic of the project, and reviews relevant concepts.

- Outcomes: Lists what students will know how to do after completing the project.

- What You'll Need: Lists specific requirements for the project.

- Completion Time: Provides an estimated completion time as a guide. (Actual completion times may vary depending on experience levels.)

- Precautions: Notes on issues that should be taken into account prior to undertaking the project.

- Projects: A variety of project types are included. The majority of projects involve hands-on activities in which students are guided through the steps required to accomplish a task. Some projects involve case-based scenarios, while others assess students' familiarity with basic concepts through matching and other paper-and-pen exercises. Many of the projects include multiple parts related to the project topic.

- Assessment Questions: Embedded within each project, these questions help students assess their understanding as they go.

- Graphic Elements: Each project contains screenshots, conceptual graphics, and/or tables that help inform and guide students as they proceed through the project.

After completing the activities in this Project Manual, students will be able to:
- install Windows Server 2003 and Windows XP Professional

- install a network adapter

- configure networking parameters

- install, configure, and run Network Monitor

- create an Active Directory domain
- determine the physical and logical network topology in use
- identify various cable types
- install and configure network protocols
- configure a host for dynamic address assignment
- configure DNS client properties
- design subnetworks to meet network configuration requirements
- configure wireless support
- enable routing and remote access
- configure a dial-up and VPN connection
- compare NOS features and characteristics
- configure Windows Server 2003 roles
- use Network Monitor and System Monitor
- identify design-phase deliverables
- identify network devices
- configure periodic backups and restore backup data
- monitor server activity
- configure Automatic Updates and automatic software distribution
- install and configure SNMP services
- configure auditing, account lockout policy, and password policy
- manage event logs
- configure computers to minimize threats

CONTENTS

Important Note about Completing the Activities in this Manual:
For all activities that require documents and other content not included in this printed project manual, please visit the book companion site indicated on the back of this manual. At the website, click on Student Companion Site in the upper right of the webpage, then Project Manual, and then the chapter in which the activity appears.

1

NETWORKING FUNDAMENTALS

PROJECTS

Project 1.1	Understanding Key Concepts
Overview	It is important to understand the basic networking standards, including the OSI, DoD, and Internet networking models. These models provide common terms for describing network operations and ways of describing and comparing network components. This project reviews common networking terms and terms relating to networking standards.
Outcomes	After completing this project, you will know how to: ▲ identify key terms and concepts related to networking basics ▲ identify key terms and concepts related to network components and network types
What you'll need	To complete this project, you will need: ▲ the worksheet below
Completion time	20 minutes
Precautions	None

The worksheet includes a list of terms related to networking standards, with models given on the left and descriptions on the right. Match each term with the description that it most closely matches. You will *not* use all descriptions. Each description can be used only once.

___ Router

___ Hub

___ Cable plant

___ Peer-to-peer

___ Wide area network

___ Client/server

___ Connection

A. Process of having two computers recognize each other and open a communication channel

B. Block of data formatted for transmission over a network

C. Transmission media and network devices making up the physical structure of a network

D. Specialized computer providing resources to a network

E. Connection device used to connect network cables at a central connection point

F. Device that enables a computer to physically connect to a network

G. Network communication device used to connect two or more networks (subnetworks or network segments)

___ Infrastructure

___ Network adapter

___ Node

___ Packet

___ Protocol

___ Ethernet

___ Server

H. Low-level protocol that is currently the protocol most commonly used

I. Rules and standards defining network communications

J. Networking model based on all network entities being tracked and managed through a directory that provides centralized management and control.

K. Networking model with no centralized security or management control

L. Any uniquely identified network device

M. Traditionally defined by LANs connected through the switched telephone network over a large geographic area

N. Path over which network devices communicate in a wired network infrastructure

O. Means by which computers identify each other on a network

P. Networking model that has centralized security control as a defining feature

Project 1.2	Identifying Basic Components
Overview	An important part of understanding network fundamentals is the ability to recognize common network components. Many connectivity components are common to the majority of PC networks.
Outcomes	After completing this project, you will know how to: ▲ recognize common network components ▲ recognize wired and wireless networks
What you'll need	To complete this project, you will need: ▲ the worksheet below
Completion time	15 minutes
Precautions	None

Match the letters to the networking terms listed under Figure 1-1. All terms will be used and each term will be used only once.

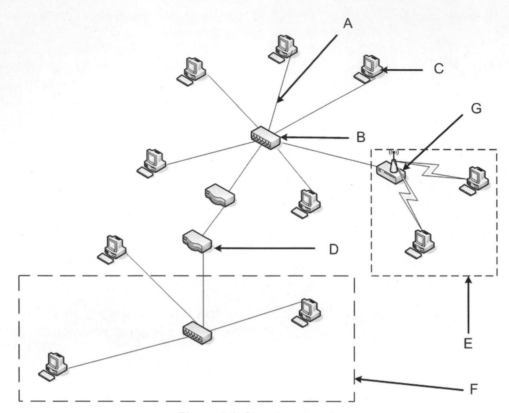

Figure 1-1: Sample network

Terms

A. _____

B. _____   Wired network

Wireless network

Hub

C. _____   Client computer

Router

D. _____   Cable plant

Wireless access point

E. _____

F. _____

G. _____

Project 1.3	Understanding Network Types
Overview	There are various ways in which you can identify and categorize networks. You can identify a network, for example, by type, architecture, and topology. Network type refers to whether the network is configured as a local, metropolitan, or wide area network. Architecture refers to the logical network design and networking model that defines features such as whether the network is based on centralized or decentralized security. Topology refers to the physical structure of the network and how network devices are connected.
	It can get complicated because these categories can be mixed and matched in a number of ways. Just because you know the network type, you don't necessarily know everything about its architecture and/or its topology.
	While each of these are important, for now we'll focus on one way of identifying networks, i.e., by network type. You need to be able to compare and contrast local area networks (LANs), metropolitan area networks (MANs), and wide area networks (WANs) to determine the best solution to an organization's needs.
Outcomes	After completing this project, you will know how to: ▲ compare and contrast network types ▲ choose a network type based on organizational requirements
What you'll need	To complete this project, you will need: ▲ the worksheet below
Completion time	60 minutes
Precautions	None

Read each of the networking scenarios and answer the questions that follow the scenario. You will be required to identify the appropriate network type and answer questions about how networking requirements might be met.

■ Part A: Networking scenario #1

All of your company's offices are located in Boston and surrounding suburbs. You need to prepare a networking solution that enables employees in all six offices to communicate both internally in that office and, to a lesser extent, between the offices. The farthest distance between any two offices is 50 miles. Most user resource requirements are met by servers located in the same office as the users who need to access them. The main communication requirements between offices relate to e-mail and periodic file transfers. You have been promised a budget sufficient to meet the requirements, but have also been told to keep costs to a minimum.

1. What network type should you use to configure the complete network?

   _____

   _____

2. What network type should you use to configure each office?

   _____

   _____

3. How many internetwork connections would you typically configure at each office?

   _____

   _____

4. What are potential concerns related to the connections between the offices?

   _____

   _____

   _____

■ Part B: Networking scenario #2

Your company occupies the top three floors of a building. Other companies have offices on the floors below you. You want to design the network to make it as easy to manage as possible. You want to minimize the potential impact of problems on any one floor to the other two floors. You are implementing this as a wired network.

1. What network type should you use to configure the complete network?

   _____

   _____

2. What network type should you use to configure each floor?

   _____

   _____

3. In general terms, describe how you would connect the floors.

   _____

   _____

   _____

4. What type of network device should you use to connect the computers on each floor?

    _____

    _____

5. What one component's failure would prevent the floors from communicating with each other? How would this impact communications between all of the computers on a single floor?

    _____

    _____

    _____

6. What role might the Internet have in this configuration?

    _____

    _____

    _____

■ Part C: Networking scenario #3

You work for a nonprofit organization with an office in each state in the continental United States. Each office provides various support services to family farms located in the state for which it is responsible. You have nearly constant interoffice communication requirements. All networking expenses must be justified to the organization's management board and you are expected to find ways to keep these expenses to a minimum.

1. What network type should you use to configure the complete network?

    _____

    _____

2. What network type should you use at each office?

    _____

    _____

3. You need to keep the equipment, service, and support costs needed to connect the offices to a minimum. Describe, in general terms, what you should use as your communication backbone between the offices. Justify your answer.

_____

_____

_____

_____

4. Other than keeping cost to a minimum, what is the primary concern for interoffice connections?

_____

_____

_____

Project 1.4	Preparing for Network Installation
Overview	Like so many other things in life, one of the fastest ways to learn the ins and outs of networking is to dive in with both hands and do it yourself. With modern technologies, all you need for a basic network is two or more computers with network adapters and appropriate operating systems and a communication path. If you're setting up a wireless network (and don't need to connect to a wired network), that's all you need. For a wired network, you also need: • a network cable for each computer • a hub, switch, or other connection device We're going to set up a wired network, so your first step is to make sure that you've made the necessary hardware connections. The project assumes that you are setting up a small, private, two-node network. If you are setting up a larger classroom network, your instructor may provide you with additional information and requirements.
Outcomes	After completing this project, you will know how to: ▲ identify minimum wired network hardware requirements ▲ install a network adapter ▲ connect a wired network
What you'll need	To complete this project, you will need: ▲ the connection instructions below ▲ two computers with Ethernet network adapters

	▲ two network cables
	▲ a hub or switch
Completion time	10 minutes
Precautions	If connecting to a classroom network, your instructor may provide alternate steps. If so, use those steps instead of the ones provided here.
	If connecting to an existing network, you *must* review what you are doing with the network administrator before making any connection to the network.
	Do not power on the computers after making the physical network connections.

Below are the steps to connect a simple Ethernet wired network. Make sure that you have the required equipment available before you start. If connecting to an existing network, provide your network administrator with a copy of these instructions so that he or she can change them as necessary to meet network requirements.

■ Part A: Install the network adapter

Complete the following steps only if a computer does not have a built-in network adapter or if the network adapter is not already installed. Each computer must have a network adapter to complete the projects in this manual. Use caution during component installation. Electronic components are easily damaged, so be careful to avoid electrostatic discharge (shock) while installing the adapter.

1. Power off and unplug the computer.
2. Remove the computer cover.
3. Locate an open PCI expansion slot.
4. Remove the slot cover and insert the network adapter, checking that it is fully seated.
5. Replace the anchor screw to hold the network adapter in place.
6. Replace the computer cover.

■ Part B: Build the network

1. Place the hub (or switch) within easy distance of both computers.
2. Connect one end of a network cable to the first open port on the hub. A sample hub with attached cables is shown in Figure 1-2.

Figure 1-2: Hub with attached cables

3. Attach the other end of the network cable to the network adapter port on the first computer, as shown in Figure 1-3.

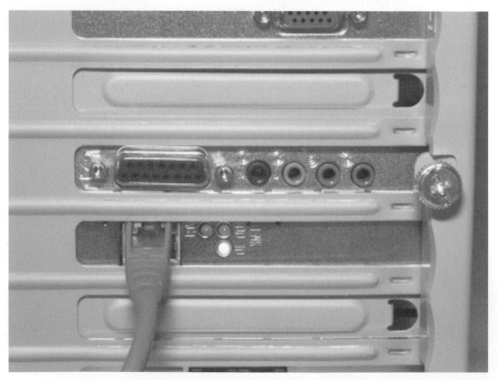

Figure 1-3: Connected network cable

4. Repeat steps 3 and 4 for the second computer.

5. Plug in the hub to AC power.

Project 1.5	Installing Windows Server 2003
Overview	Microsoft Windows Server 2003 is a version of Microsoft's server operating system. It can be used in a server-only role or as a peer server where it is used as both a client and a server. You will be prompted for network configuration information during Windows Server 2003 installation. You can set configuration parameters at that time, but you also have the option of going back and changing your network configuration as needed.
Outcomes	After completing this project, you will know how to: ▲ install Windows Server 2003 ▲ configure networking parameters ▲ verify successful installation
What you'll need	To complete this project, you will need: ▲ Project 1.4 completed ▲ Windows Server 2003 installation CD
Completion time	60 minutes (approximate, depending on computer configuration and speed)
Precautions	The instructions in this project assume you will be setting up a two-node network with one computer running Windows XP Professional and one computer running Windows Server 2003. If you are deploying the Windows Server 2003 computer as part of a larger classroom network, your instructor will provide you with alternate instructions for configuring network parameters. If you are adding the Windows Server 2003 computer to an existing network, you should also review the project steps with your network administrator. Your network administrator may need to make changes or additions to the installation instructions.

■ Part A: Prepare for installation

This project provides the instructions for installing Windows Server 2003 from the installation CD and configuring networking parameters. Required parameters include the computer name and TCP/IP address parameters. Your instructor may provide alternate values for some configuration parameters. If so, record those below:

Computer name: _____

IP address: _____

Subnet mask: _____

This project assumes that you will be configuring the computer with a single disk partition. If your computer needs to be configured differently, your instructor will provide you with alternate partitioning instructions. These will replace steps 4 through 7 below.

■ Part B: Install Windows Server 2003

Complete the following steps to install Windows Server 2003. These steps assume that there is no operating system currently installed on the computer. You may not understand some of the prompts during installation, but just follow the specific installation instructions provided here.

1. Power up the computer, insert the installation CD, and boot from the installation CD. With most computers, you will see a prompt **Press any key to boot from CD**. Press any key when prompted.

2. When the **Windows Server 2003 Setup** screen opens, the edition you are installing (Standard, Enterprise, Web, etc.) is shown. Depending on the licensing arrangement, you may also see a message telling you that you have only a certain period of time in which to activate the installation. Press Enter. The Setup program then begins loading the necessary files for the GUI portion of the installation.

3. After the files have loaded, the **Welcome to Setup** screen appears (Figure 1-4). When prompted, press Enter to start the installation.

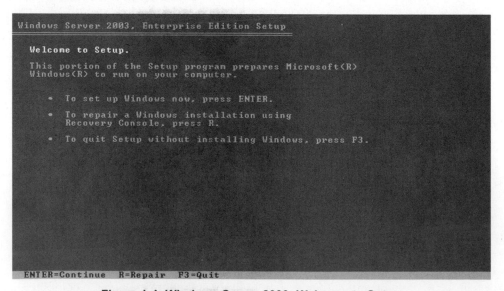

Figure 1-4: Windows Server 2003: Welcome to Setup

4. The **Windows Licensing Agreement** screen opens. Press F8 to accept the License Agreement.

5. Unless otherwise specified by your instructor, when prompted to select an installation destination, press Enter to accept the default destination.

6. If prompted, press C to continue the installation. You should see this only if there is an operating system already installed on the computer.

7. When prompted to choose your format option, select to format the partition using the **NTFS** file system and press Enter to start the format.

8. If prompted, press F to verify your selection and start the physical format.

   Depending on hard disk size, the format process may take several minutes. After format is complete, Setup will automatically copy the installation files to the hard disk and restart the computer. You can remove the installation CD at this time. *Do not* choose to boot from the installation CD. Installation will continue after the computer restarts from the hard disk.

9. The **Regional and Language Options** screen opens. When prompted with the default regional and language selections, click Next to continue without making any changes.

10. The **Personalize Your Software** screen appears. Type your name and the name **Busicorp** (without quotes) as the organizational name, and click Next to continue.

11. The **Your Product Key** screen opens. Enter the product key value for this copy of Windows XP Professional, and click Next to continue. If you are using an evaluation copy, you will not be prompted for the product key.

12. The **Licensing Modes** screen appears (Figure 1-5). Click Next to accept the default license mode (per server licensing) and continue.

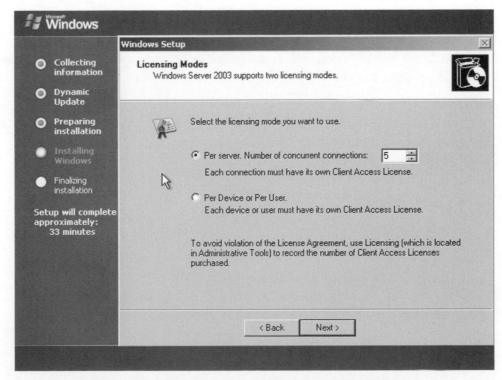

Figure 1-5: Windows Server 2003: Setup/Licensing Modes

13. The **Computer Name and Administrator Password** screen opens. Unless provided with an alternate computer name by your instructor or network administrator, enter the following information and then click Next to continue.

    Computer name: **MainServer00**

    Password: **P*ssword**

    Confirm password: **P*ssword**

14. If a modem is detected, the **Modem Dialing Information** screen opens. Enter the necessary information including the area code or city code, if necessary, and then click Next. This screen is omitted if the computer does not have a modem

15. The **Date and Time Settings** screen opens. Select your local time zone and click Next to continue. There will be a delay while the computer prepares to install networking.

16. The **Networking Settings** screen opens. When prompted for network settings, select **Custom Settings** and click Next.

17. Select **Internet Protocol (TCP/IP)** and click **Properties**.

18. Unless provided with alternate address parameters by your instructor or network administrator, enter the following:

    IP address: **192.168.1.11**

    Subnet mask: **255.255.255.0**

19. Leave the remaining prompts at their defaults and click OK.

20. Click Next to continue.

21. The **Workgroup or Computer Domain** screen opens. Type **BUSICORPWG** as the workgroup name and click Next to continue.

22. The computer will restart automatically when setup is complete and the **Welcome to Microsoft Windows Server 2003** initial logon screen will appear (Figure 1-6).

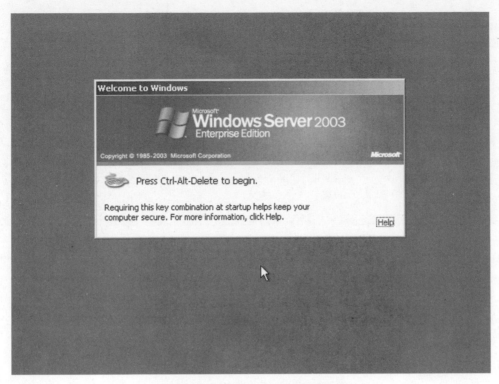

Figure 1-6: Welcome to Windows

■ Part C: Verify installation

1. Press Ctrl + Alt + Del to open the **Log on to Windows** dialog box.
2. When the logon screen displays, log on as **Administrator** using the password specified during installation.
3. If prompted to adjust screen resolution, follow the on-screen prompts to complete the process.
4. Open the **Start** menu, point to **All Programs** and then to **Accessories**, and then select **Command Prompt** to open a **Command Prompt** window.
5. Type **ipconfig** and press Enter.
6. Verify that the computer name and IP address reported are the same as the address specified during installation.
7. Type **exit** and press Enter to close the **Command Prompt** window.
8. Open the **Start** menu and select **Shut Down**. When prompted, type a reason for shutting down in the **Comment** prompt and click OK.

2

NETWORK STANDARDS AND MODELS

PROJECTS

Project 2.1	Understanding Key Concepts
Overview	Today, manufacturers design and build PCs and operating systems with the assumption that they'll be deployed in a network environment. Because of this, it's important that you understand network fundamentals, beginning with fundamental terms and concepts.
Outcomes	After completing this project, you will know how to: ▲ identify key terms and concepts related to models and standards ▲ identify key terms and concepts related to the OSI and Internet networking models
What you'll need	To complete this project, you will need: ▲ the worksheet below
Completion time	20 minutes
Precautions	None

The worksheet includes a list of networking terms on the left and descriptions on the right. Match each term with the description that it most closely matches. You will *not* use all descriptions. Each description can be used only once.

____   Connectionless transmission

A. Process of inserting markers into data packets to enable a conversation to continue after errors

____   Flow control

B. Communication sessions using connection-oriented transmissions

____   Logical address

C. Two-way data communication where both ends can transmit simultaneously

____   MAC address

D. Transmission method where the receiving system does not acknowledge receipt of data

____   Hop

E. Standard developed and accepted through use and application

____   Ethernet

F. TCP/IP suite protocol used to access web pages

____   Data compression

G. Method of ensuring that data sent to the recipient is in a format that the recipient can process

___ Data encryption

H. Address assigned to a computer through networking software and uniquely identifying the computer to the network

___ Header

I. Standard developed by an official body

___ Reliable transport method

J. Using algorithms to modify data from being ready by anyone other than the sender and intended recipient

___ Data presentation

K. Router passed through during packet routing

___ HTTP

L. Common term for the IEEE 802.3 networking standard

___ Formal standard

M. Term used to refer to data packets at the OSI network layer

___ De facto standard

N. Act of physically shrinking data to minimize network traffic

___ Routing

O. Communication control that prevents a computer from being overwhelmed by incoming traffic

___ Full-duplex communication

P. Information added to describe a data packet, including source and destination computers

Q. Process of directing packets though an internetwork to the correct destination network

R. Network device address that is hard coded on the network adapter

Project 2.2	Comparing Network Models
Overview	Standards can be developed by a formal standards organization or come into being through common acceptance and use. Standards have been an important part of network design and development. They help to ensure interoperability between different manufacturers' products. They provide standard, accepted terms for describing network functions and network activity. In short, they provide a standard language for discussing networking. Three common network model standards are the OSI model, the DoD model, and the Internet model. You need to understand each of these models, how they are structured, and what occurs at each level.

Outcomes	After completing this project, you will know how to:
	▲ identify network model layered structures
	▲ recognize activities occurring at different model layers
What you'll need	To complete this project, you will need:
	▲ the worksheet below
Completion time	45 minutes
Precautions	None

■ Part A: Identify model layers

In Figure 2-1, fill in the names for each of the model layers in their correct positions. The names are listed below the figure. All names will be used. Each name may be used more than once.

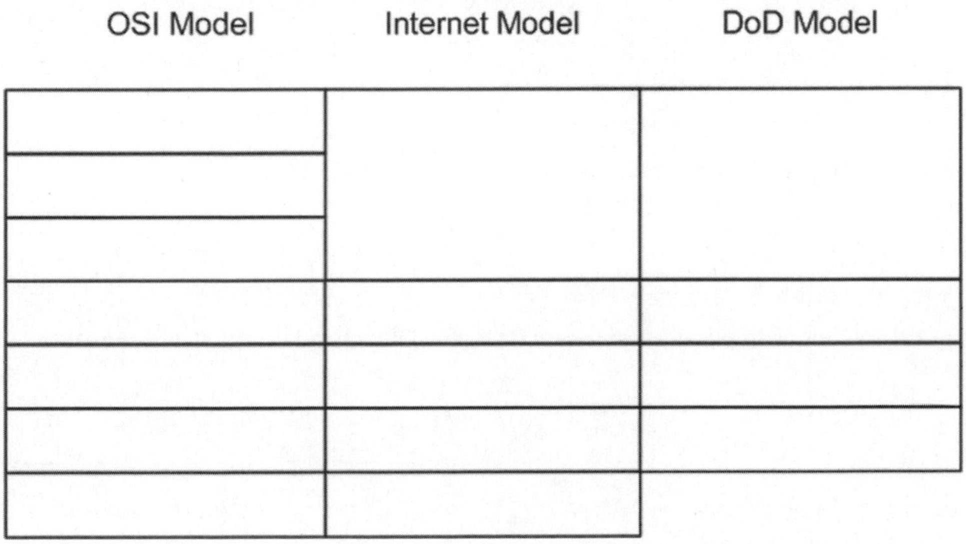

Figure 2-1: Networking models

Application	Physical
Data Link	Presentation
Host-to-Host	Process
Internet	Session
Network	Transport
Network Interface	

■ Part B: Understand layer use

The following questions refer to network technologies and their relationship with the OSI, DoD, and Internet network models. Answer each question and briefly explain why your answer is correct.

1. Why can it be said that the NetBEUI protocol does not implement the OSI model Network layer?

    _____

    _____

    _____

2. Which layer in the OSI and Internet models is not considered a layer in the DoD model?

    _____

    _____

3. At which layer are Ethernet and WiFi implemented in the OSI model?

    _____

    _____

4. Into what sublayers is the OSI model Data Link layer is divided?

    _____

    _____

5. In the OSI model, with what other layers does the Transport layer directly interface?

    _____

    _____

6. During the routing process, while passing through a router, datagrams pass through which layers of the Internet model?

    _____

    _____

7. Which two protocols in the TCP/IP protocol suite operate at the Host-to-Host layer of the DoD model?

    _____

    _____

8. Tools that translate an Internet Universal Resource Locator (URL) address to a numeric IP address are provided at which layer of the OSI model?

_____

_____

9. What is the relationship between the OSI, DoD, and Internet model Application layers?

_____

_____

_____

10. At which layer are IP addresses defined in the DoD model?

_____

_____

Project 2.3	Installing Windows XP Professional
Overview	Microsoft Windows XP Professional is one of the most popular choices for network clients. Other versions designed specifically for home use, Windows XP Home and Windows XP Media Center Edition, are the operating systems currently most often found on home networks. One of the keys to having a reliable network is proper installation of client software, in this case, Windows XP Professional. You are prompted for network configuration information during Windows XP installation. You can set configuration parameters at that time, but you also have the option of going back and changing your network configuration as needed.
Outcomes	After completing this project, you will know how to: ▲ install Windows XP Professional ▲ configure networking parameters ▲ verify successful installation
What you'll need	To complete this project, you will need: ▲ network cable plant and connection devices installed (or Project 1.4 completed) ▲ a Windows XP Professional installation CD
Completion time	60 minutes (approximate, depending on computer configuration and speed)
Precautions	The instructions in this project assume you will be setting up a two-node network with one computer running Windows XP Professional and one computer running Windows Server 2003. If you are deploying the Windows XP computer as part of a larger classroom network, your

instructor will provide you with alternate instructions for configuring network parameters.

If you are adding the Windows XP computer to an existing network, you should also review the project steps with your network administrator. Your network administrator may need to make changes or additions to the installation instructions.

■ Part A: Prepare for installation

This project provides instructions for installing Windows XP Professional from the installation CD and configuring networking parameters. Required parameters include the computer name and TCP/IP address parameters. Your instructor may provide alternate values for some configuration parameters. If so, record those below:

Computer name: _____

IP address: _____

Subnet mask: _____

This project assumes that you will be configuring the computer with a single disk partition. If your computer needs to be configured differently, your instructor will provide you with alternate partitioning instructions. These will replace steps 4 through 7 below.

■ Part B: Install Windows XP Professional

Complete the following steps to install Windows XP Professional. These steps assume that there is no operating system currently installed on the computer. You may not understand some of the prompts during installation, but just follow the specific installation instructions provided here.

1. Power up the computer, insert the installation CD, and boot from the installation CD. With most computers, you will see a prompt **Press any key to boot from CD**. Press any key when prompted.

2. The **Welcome to Setup** screen appears (Figure 2-2). Press Enter to start the installation.

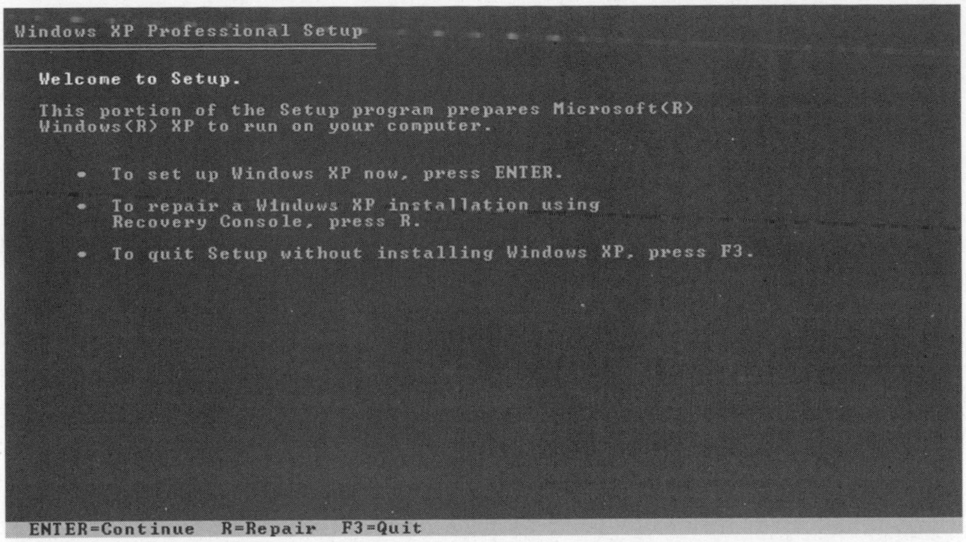

```
Windows XP Professional Setup

  Welcome to Setup.

  This portion of the Setup program prepares Microsoft(R)
  Windows(R) XP to run on your computer.

     •  To set up Windows XP now, press ENTER.

     •  To repair a Windows XP installation using
        Recovery Console, press R.

     •  To quit Setup without installing Windows XP, press F3.




  ENTER=Continue   R=Repair   F3=Quit
```

Figure 2-2: Windows XP: Welcome to Setup screen

3. The **License Agreement** screen opens. Scroll down to the bottom of the page and press F8 to accept the License Agreement.

4. Unless otherwise specified by your instructor, when prompted to select an installation destination, press Enter to accept the default destination.

5. If prompted, press C to continue the installation. This prompt appears only if there is an operating system already installed on the computer

6. When prompted to choose your format option, select to format the partition using the **NTFS** file system and press Enter to start the format.

7. If prompted, press F to verify your selection and start the physical format. Depending on hard disk size, the format process may take several minutes. After format is complete, Setup will automatically copy the installation files to the hard disk and restart the computer. You can remove the installation CD at this time. *Do not* choose to boot from the installation CD. Installation will continue after the computer restarts from the hard disk.

8. The **Regional and Language Options** screen opens. Verify that the settings are correct and click Next to continue.

9. The **Personalize Your Software** screen appears (Figure 2-3). Type your name and the name **Busicorp** as the organizational name, and click Next to continue.

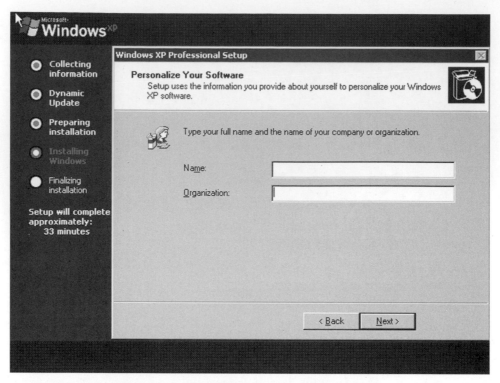

Figure 2-3: Personalize Your Software screen

10. The **Your Product Key** screen appears. Enter the product key value for this copy of Windows XP Professional and click Next to continue. If you are using an evaluation copy, you will not be prompted for the product key.

11. The **Computer Name and Administrator Password** screen opens. Unless provided with an alternate computer name by your instructor or network administrator, enter the following information and then click Next to continue:

    Computer name: **Student00**

    Password: **P*ssword**

    Confirm password: **P*ssword**

    Each computer on the network must have a unique name.

12. If you have a Plug-and-Play modem installed, the **Modem Dialing Information** screen will appear. Specify the settings for your environment and click Next.

13. Select your local time zone in the **Date and Time Settings** screen and click Next to continue. There will be a delay while the computer prepares to install networking.

14. The **Network Settings** screen opens. When prompted for network settings, select **Custom Settings** and click Next.

15. Select **Internet Protocol (TCP/IP)** and click **Properties**.

16. Unless provided with alternate address parameters by your instructor or network administrator, enter the following:

    IP address: **192.168.1.21**

    Subnet mask: **255.255.255.0**

Each computer in a TCP/IP network must have a unique address. If a duplicate address is detected during start-up, the computer will disable TCP/IP networking until the problem is corrected.

17. Leave the remaining prompts at their defaults and click OK.

18. Click Next to continue.

19. The **Workgroup or Computer Domain** screen appears. Select the **No, This Computer Is Not on a Network, or Is on a Network without a Domain** option button, if necessary, to indicate that you do not want to join a domain. Type **BUSICORPWG** as the workgroup name and click Next to continue. The computer will restart automatically when setup is complete.

■ Part C: Verify installation

1. When the **Welcome** screen displays, select the **Administrator** account, type the password and press Enter.

2. If prompted to adjust screen resolution, follow the on-screen prompts to complete the process.

3. Open the **Start** menu, point to **All Programs** and then to **Accessories**, and then select **Command Prompt** to open a command prompt window.

4. Type **ipconfig** and press Enter.

5. Verify that the computer name and IP address reported are the same as the values specified during installation.

6. Type **exit** and press Enter to close the **Command Prompt** window.

7. Open the **Start** menu and select **Turn Off Computer**. Select **Turn Off** when prompted to shut down the computer.

Project 2.4	Installing Windows XP Service Pack 2
Overview	Microsoft periodically releases fixes, security patches, and updates to its applications and operating systems. One way it does this is through service packs, which include a collection of changes and updates for the product for which it is created. Windows XP Service Pack 2 was seen as an especially important release because of additional features and functionality it provides, including improved wireless support and release of the Windows Security Center.
	When installing a service pack for an application or operating system, it is necessary to install only the most recent service pack. The most recent version of the service pack will include all of the updates released in prior versions. In other words, Service Pack 2 also includes updates released with Service Pack 1, so there is no need to install Service Pack 1 before installing Service Pack 2.

	Typically, if there is a service pack available, you will apply it immediately after installing the operating system. If one becomes available after the operating system is installed, it is recommended that you install it as soon as it is convenient and make a special effort to install it as soon as possible if you have experienced any of the problems corrected by the service pack.
	Microsoft makes released service pack versions available for download from its website. For most products, including current Windows operating system versions, you can request the current service pack on CD for a small charge.
Outcomes	After completing this project, you will know how to: ▲ apply Windows XP Service Pack 2 ▲ verify the current service pack version
What you'll need	To complete this project, you will need: ▲ a computer with Windows XP Professional installed ▲ Windows XP Service Pack 2 installation CD
Completion time	30 minutes (approximate, varies by computer)
Precautions	You must complete Project 2.3, in which you install Windows XP Professional, before starting this project. If your computer is part of a network other than a dedicated or private training network, you should check with your network administrator before making any changes.

Below are the steps to install Windows XP Service Pack 2 from CD. If installing from a source other than CD, your instructor will provide you with alternate installation steps.

■ Part A: Install Service Pack 2

1. If not already running, start the computer with Windows XP Professional installed and log on as Administrator.
2. Insert the **Windows XP Service Pack 2** installation CD.
3. When prompted with the **Welcome** menu screen, click Continue.
4. Click Install Now. **Setup** extracts the files it needs for installation before launching the **Setup** wizard.
5. When the **Setup Wizard Welcome** screen displays, as shown in Figure 2-4, click Next to start installation.

Figure 2-4: Service Pack Setup Wizard

6. Review the License Agreement, select **I Agree,** and click Next to continue.

7. Click Next to accept the default uninstall folder and continue. Replaced files are written to the uninstall folder, which makes it possible to uninstall the changes made during service pack installation.

8. Installation begins automatically after you click Next. Service Pack installation can take several minutes, depending on computer speed and configuration. *Do not* click Cancel while Setup is running. This will abort the service pack installation.

9. When Setup is complete, click Finish. *Do not* select **Do not restart now**. The computer will restart automatically. If the computer does not restart automatically, open the **Start** menu, select **Turn Off Computer** and then select **Restart** to restart the computer manually.

■ **Part B: Verify installation**

1. After restart, you will be prompted to turn on **Automatic Updates**. Select **Not right now** and click Next.

2. Log on as **Administrator**.

3. The **Windows Security Center**, as shown in Figure 2-5, launches automatically. Click the red X in the upper-right corner of the **Windows Security Center** window to exit the **Security Center**.

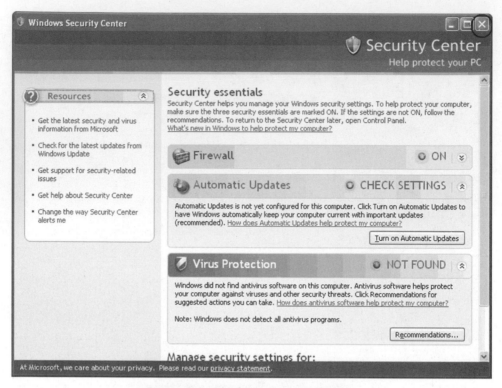

Figure 2-5: Windows Security Center

4. Click Start and then select **Control Panel**.

5. In the menu on the left, under **Control Panel**, click Switch to Classic View to change to **Classic View**.

6. Double-click **System** to open the **System Properties** dialog box. What is reported as the current service pack version?

_____

7. Select the **Automatic Updates** tab. How are **Automatic Updates** currently configured?

_____

_____

8. Click Cancel to exit the **System Properties** dialog box without making any changes.

Project 2.5	Mapping Network Components
Overview	Microsoft and other operating system manufacturers build network components into their operating systems. You can view and manage the status of these networking components. Many components also have parameters that you can configure to control how your computer communicates on the network.

	Part of understanding these network components is knowing how they are related to each other. One way to do this is to map them to the appropriate network model layers. The standard model, even though it is not strictly adhered to by most manufacturers, is the OSI model. Other common models are the DoD model, which is also known as the TCP/IP model, and the Internet model. The DoD and Internet models are very similar, but do have two differences. The DoD model does not include a Physical layer. Also, the layers are named differently, even though the layers in both the DoD and Internet models map to the same layers in the OSI model. The layers supported by both of these models are functionally identical.
Outcomes	After completing this project, you will know how to: ▲ view networking components and parameters
What you'll need	To complete this project, you will need: ▲ the following worksheet ▲ a computer running Windows XP Professional with service pack 2
Completion time	60 minutes
Precautions	Do not make any changes to the computer's configuration unless explicitly told to do so by the project steps. Otherwise, you will view only configuration parameters during this project. You should be logged on as Administrator before starting this project.

This project assumes that the Control Panel is configured to show selections in Classic View, as configured in Project 2.4. If not, you should configure the Control Panel for Classic View before you start. The project steps will direct you to display various network components and configuration parameters. You will also be asked to display the model layer to which the item belongs. For each component, identify the appropriate OSI, DoD, and Internet model layers and justify your selection.

1. Open the **Start** menu and select **Control Panel**. If currently configured for the category view, change to Classic View.

2. Double-click **Network Connections** to open the **Network Connections** window.

3. Right-click your local connection and select **Properties** to open the **Local Area Connection Properties** dialog box, as shown in Figure 2-6.

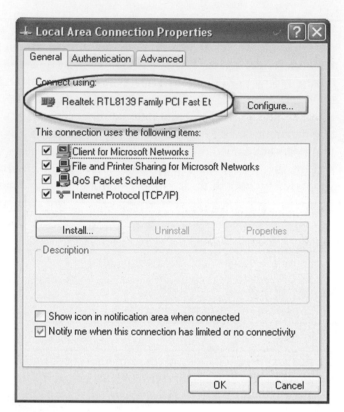

Figure 2-6: Local Area Connection Properties dialog box

4. Select **Internet Protocol (TCP/IP)** and click Properties.

5. With which layer is this IP address information associated?

   OSI model: _____

   DoD model: _____

   Internet model: _____

6. Click Cancel to close the **Internet Protocol (TCP/IP) Properties** dialog box and then Cancel to close the **Local Area Connection Properties** dialog box. Close the **Network Connections** window.

7. Open a **Command Prompt** window, type **ipconfig**, and press Enter. How does the information reported compare to that in the **Internet Protocol (TCP/IP) Properties** dialog box?

   _____

   _____

8. What is the IP address?

   _____

9. Type **ipconfig /all** in the **Command Prompt** window. What is the physical address value?

   _____

10. In what numbering system is this reported?

_____

11. With which network model layer is this value associated?

    OSI model: _____

    DoD model: _____

    Internet model: _____

12. Close the **Command Prompt** window.

13. Open the **Start** menu and select **Internet** to launch the default web browser, **Internet Explorer**. If configured with Internet access, the default **Home page** will display. If not, the warning shown in Figure 2-7 displays.

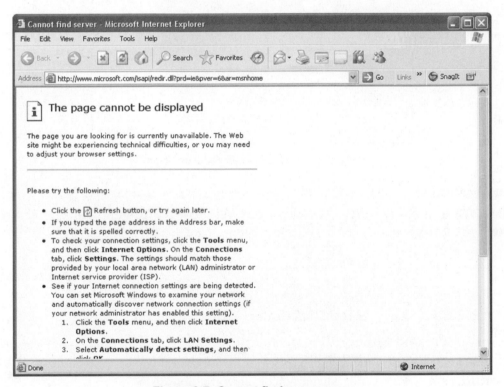

Figure 2-7: Cannot find server error

14. With which network model layer is this application associated?

    OSI model: _____

    DoD model: _____

    Internet model: _____

15. Open the **Control Panel** and launch **Windows Firewall**. **Windows Firewall** should be configured as shown in Figure 2-8.

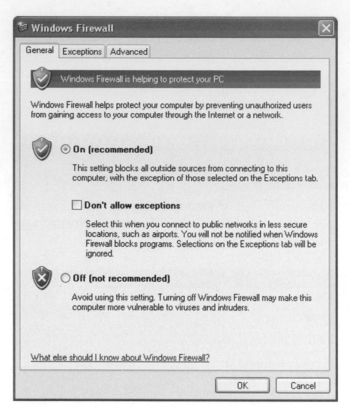

Figure 2-8: Windows Firewall enabled

16. If not configured as in Figure 2-8, change your configuration to match the figure.

17. Click **What else should I know about Windows Firewall**. What protections are listed? What risks not blocked by Windows Firewall are listed?

    _____

    _____

    _____

18. Close the **Help and Support Center** window.

19. Select the **Exceptions** tab in the **Windows Firewall** dialog box, select **File and Printer Sharing**, and click Edit. For what protocols are exceptions listed?

    _____

    _____

20. With which network model layer are these protocols associated?

    OSI model: _____

    DoD model: _____

    Internet model: _____

21. Click **Cancel** to close the **Edit** dialog box and then click **Cancel** to close **the Windows Firewall** dialog box.

Project 2.6	Capturing Network Traffic
Overview	Microsoft Windows Server 2003 ships with the Network Monitor utility, which enables you to capture and view network traffic. Network Monitor does not install by default, but can be added to your computer by installing the optional Support tools from the installation CD. The version of Network Monitor that ships with Windows Server 2003 is somewhat limited in that it can capture only traffic going into or out of the computer on which it is running. An enhanced version of Network Monitor ships with Microsoft Systems Management Server that lets you capture, store, and view all network traffic. After capturing network traffic, you can view the contents of individual packets. This will let you see how the packet is formatted and identify components added at various levels in the OSI model.
Outcomes	After completing this project, you will know how to: ▲ install, configure, and run Network Monitor ▲ capture, sort, and view network traffic ▲ view the contents of network packets
What you'll need	To complete this project, you will need: ▲ a computer with Windows Server 2003 installed ▲ Windows Server 2003 installation CD
Completion time	60 minutes (approximate, depending on computer configuration and speed)
Precautions	If your computer is part of a network other than a dedicated or private training network, you should check with your network administrator before making any changes or before running Network Monitor to capture network traffic. Network Monitor, if misused, is a potential security risk because of the information that can be collected from network packets. You will need the IP address and MAC address information collected in the Project 2.5 to complete this project.

■ Part A: Install Network Monitor

1. Open the **Start** menu, select **Control Panel** and then **Add or Remove Programs**, and then select **Add/Remove Windows Components**.
2. Locate and select **Management and Monitoring Tools** (Figure 2-9) and then click Details.

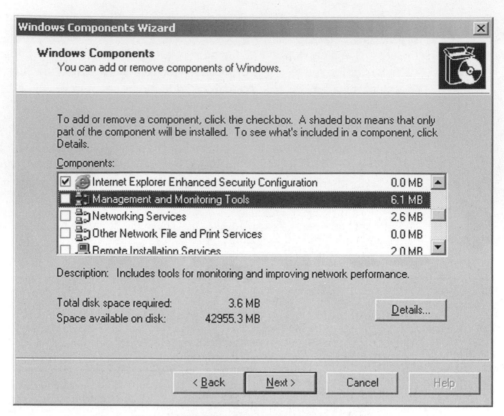

Figure 2-9: Windows Components screen

3. Select **Network Monitor Tools**, as shown in Figure 2-10, and click OK.

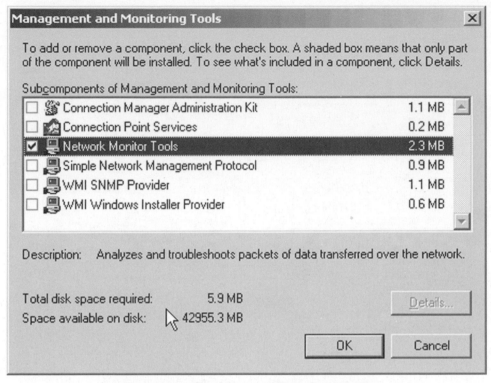

Figure 2-10: Network Monitor Tools selected

4. Click Next.

5. When prompted, insert the Windows Server 2003 installation CD. If the warning dialog box, as shown in Figure 2-11, displays, select the **In the future, do not show this message** check box and click OK to close the warning dialog box.

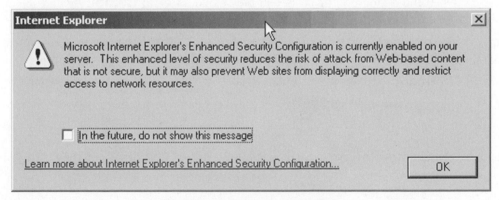

Figure 2-11: Warning dialog box

6. Click Finish.

7. Close the **Add or Remove Programs** window.

■ Part B: Capture network traffic

1. Open the **Start** menu, select **Administrative Tools** and then select **Network Monitor** to launch **Network Monitor** (Figure 2-12).

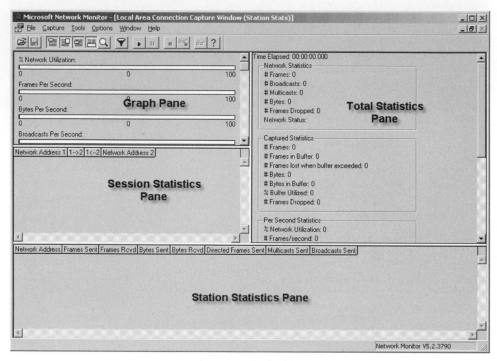

Figure 2-12: Network Monitor

2. You might be prompted to select the network on which you want to capture traffic. If you do, click OK when the dialog box displays and then expand **Local Computer** and select **Local Area Connection**. Click OK after making your selection.

3. Some of the commands and options listed in **Network Monitor** as supported only with the version that ships with Systems Management Server and are *not* supported in this version.

4. Open a **Command Prompt** and enter **ipconfig /all**. What is the computer's physical address?

_____

5. Select **Network Monitor** as the active window. Select **Capture** and then **Start** or press F10. What happens?

_____

6. Select **Command Prompt** as the active window. Type **ping *IP_Address***, replacing ***IP_Address*** with the IP address for your computer. Refer to Project 2.4 for this information, if necessary.

7. Select **Network Monitor** as the active window. Select **Capture** and then **Stop** or press F11.

8. Refer to the **Graph** pane (as shown in Figure 2-12) for communication statistics. What is the number of average frames per second? What is the average bytes per second?

    _____

    _____

9. Select **Capture** and then **Display captured data**. This will open a window similar to the example shown in Figure 2-13.

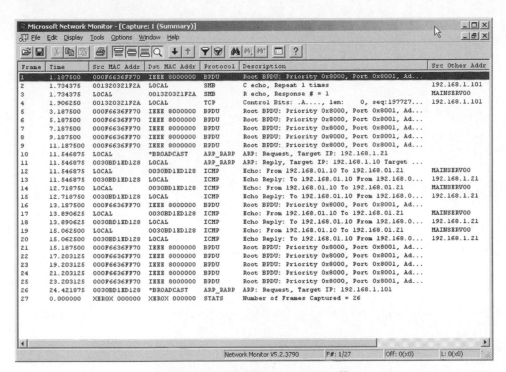

Figure 2-13: Sample captured traffic

10. Locate a frame with your Windows XP computer's MAC address in the Src MAC Addr column and ICMP as the protocol. What is the value in the Dest MAC Addr column?

    _____

11. Right-click and choose to edit this address. What is the numeric address and from where is this address taken?

    _____

12. At which layer in the OSI model are these addresses managed?

    _____

13. Exit **Network Monitor** and close the open **Command Prompt** window. If prompted, do not save the network capture.

3
NETWORK ARCHITECTURES

PROJECTS

Project 3.1	Understanding Key Concepts
Overview	There are several ways in which you might describe a network. One is by the network architecture, which describes the network's logical design and can act as a blueprint for building your network.
	Because term definitions can sometimes vary based on the context in which they are used, it is important to be able to recognize terms and how they are used in the context of network architecture.
Outcomes	After completing this project, you will know how to:
	▲ identify key terms and concepts related to network architecture
What you'll need	To complete this project, you will need:
	▲ the worksheet below
Completion time	20 minutes
Precautions	None

The worksheet includes a list of networking terms on the left and descriptions on the right. Match each term with the description that it most closely matches. You will use all descriptions. Each description can be used only once.

___ Domain	A. Any server that provides resources to a network
___ Resource server	B. Large network containing multiple servers and typically integrating wide area links
___ Network topology	C. Network architecture with no centralized security and each computer can act as both a client and a server
___ Spooler file	D. Network segment that is isolated from the rest of a physical network by a firewall
___ Workgroup	E. Logical security boundary in a directory-based network
___ Screened subnet	F. Network architecture based on a combination of standard network architectures
___ Active Directory	G. File that acts as the print queue on a print server

___ Enterprise network

H. Physical network division within a larger physical network

___ Host-based network

I. Network architecture based on a centralized model for data storage and network management

___ Hybrid network

J. Microsoft's directory-based network architecture

___ Peer-to-peer network

K. Network security device that filters traffic into and out of a network or subnet

___ Client/server network

L. Network architecture based on a mainframe or other computer with connected terminals

___ Subnetwork

M. Physical network design describing how network devices connect

___ Firewall

N. Logical peer-to-peer network grouping

Project 3.2	Comparing Network Architectures
Overview	The three network architectural models currently used in network design are peer-to-peer, client/server (or server-based), and directory services (or directory based). While peer-to-peer networks are still often found in smaller companies, many larger companies have shifted from the client/server model to the directory services model. Peer-to-peer networking is the model almost exclusively used when setting up home networks.
	It is important to realize that the network's physical layout does not in itself determine the architectural model. Often, given a schematic drawing of the physical layout, any one of the three common models could apply. Other issues such as the number of network users, resource requirements, and security needs must be considered.
	You should be able to compare and contrast these networking models. Many features are common to two or more of the architectural models, while there are other features that are unique to and help to define each of the models. A good understanding of these features and how they are related to the different models will help you choose the right model when designing or updating a network.
Outcomes	After completing this project, you will know how to: ▲ recognize network architectural model features

	▲ compare and contrast common architectural models
What you'll need	To complete this project, you will need: ▲ the worksheet below
Completion time	30 minutes
Precautions	None

Read each of the networking scenarios and answer the questions that follow the scenario.

■ Part A: Networking scenario #1

Your company has over 2000 employees and grows at an average rate of 50 employees per month. You have offices at five different locations spread across the United States. You plan to use secure connections established through high-speed Internet connections as your communications backbone between the offices. Network users will need easy access to shared resources, primarily shared files and printers. Security is not an overriding concern.

1. Which network architecture would be most appropriate in this situation? Give at least two reasons for your choice.

   _____

   _____

   _____

   _____

2. What should you use as your guideline for placing resource servers?

   _____

   _____

   _____

3. Justify using the Internet instead of connections leased from regional telephone companies to connect the office locations.

   _____

   _____

   _____

4. Does the network in this scenario qualify as an enterprise network?   Why or why not?

_____

_____

_____

5. How do security requirements impact your architecture selection?

_____

_____

_____

_____

■ Part B: Networking scenario #2

You have six users, all of whom are relatively computer literate, working from a single location. The users need to work together on projects that include multiple elements, including text documents, digital photos, and multimedia elements. Individual elements should remain local to the user who originally created the content until you are ready to produce the finished project. At that time, all of the elements are copied to one computer for final rendering. The network will not connect to the Internet and you are not worried about internal security. Users must be able to freely share and access data.

1. Which one network architecture is the best match in this situation and why? Why wouldn't you want to use one of the other architecture models in this scenario?

_____

_____

_____

_____

2. What are some of the potential hidden costs in your decision?

_____

_____

_____

_____

3. All of the computers are running Windows XP Professional, Windows 2000 Professional, or Windows Server 2003. What, if any, additional software would be required in this scenario?

_____

_____

_____

_____

4. Is computer literacy an issue in this scenario? Why or why not?

_____

_____

_____

_____

■ Part C: Networking scenario #3

You need to support 60 users in two locations. There will be a full-time connection between the locations. Because of the available bandwidth, you want to keep the traffic between the locations to a minimum. You plan to deploy a file server and print server in each location. You also need to deploy a database server, but because of the software costs involved, you will have only one database server.

1. Which network architectures could support the configuration requirements?

_____

_____

_____

2. What can you do to minimize traffic requirements during user login?

_____

_____

_____

3. How can you determine the best location for the database server?

_____

_____

_____

4. How can you justify putting file and print servers in both locations?

_____

_____

_____

5. If you configure this network as an Active Directory domain, how would this impact traffic across the link?

_____

_____

_____

■ Part D: Networking scenario #4

You need to support 20 users in three locations. There are 5 employees in the Chicago office, 6 in the St. Louis office, and 9 in the Dallas office. Chicago and St. Louis connect to Dallas through dial-up router connections that provide connectivity on an as-needed basis. Each office also connects to the Internet through a high-speed, full-time connection. Security is a primary concern and access to shared resources must be strictly controlled.

1. Which network architectures could support the configuration requirements? Why would you use these and not the other available architecture(s)?

_____

_____

_____

2. How can you improve connectivity between the locations using the resources that are currently available?

_____

_____

_____

3. A user in Chicago needs to access data on a file server located in St. Louis. Trace the path from Chicago to St. Louis that the data must take, based on the current connection. What types of problems might you encounter?

_____

_____

_____

_____

Project 3.3	Exploring a Peer-to-Peer Network
Overview	The defining feature of a peer-to-peer network is that there is no centralized resource or security management. A peer-to-peer network is designed to let users share resources from their computers and manage access security, if any, themselves. The procedures for sharing resources are somewhat operating system and version specific. The basic procedures are similar for different Windows versions, but you will see variations. For example, Windows 95 and Windows 98 support share-level security where you define the access level and a password for resource access when your share a resource to the network. This security method is not supported by later Windows versions. During this project you will explore different procedures for sharing resources from a computer running Windows XP Professional. As a test of your success, you will attempt to access the resources from another computer.
Outcomes	After completing this project, you will know how to: ▲ enable or disable Simple File Sharing ▲ share resources to the network from Windows XP Professional ▲ access shared resources
What you'll need	To complete this project, you will need: ▲ the worksheet below ▲ peer-to-peer network with Windows XP and Windows Server 2003 peer servers
Completion time	45 minutes
Precautions	If your computer is part of a network other than a dedicated or private training network, you should check with your network administrator before attempting this project and have your network administrator review the project steps. Your network administrator may find it necessary to modify the project steps.

You should be logged on as Administrator on your Windows XP and Windows Server 2003 computers.

■ Part A: Explore file sharing with Simple File Sharing enabled

Complete all project steps in this part on the computer running Windows XP Professional.

1. Open the **Start** menu and select **My Computer**.

2. Open the **Tools** menu and select **Folder Options**.

3. Select the **View** tab and scroll to the bottom of the **View Properties** dialog box. **Use simple file sharing (Recommended)** should be checked, as shown in Figure 3-1.

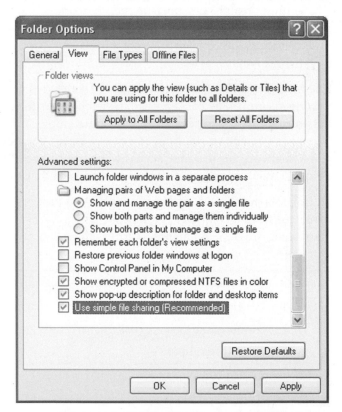

Figure 3-1: Simple File Sharing enabled

4. Click OK.

5. Open the **C:** drive, and select **File**, then **New**, and then **Folder** to create a new folder. Name the folder **Simple1.**

6. Create a second folder at the root of the **C:** drive named **Simple2**.

7. Open **Simple1**, and select **File**, then **New**, and then **Text Document**. Name the document **Limited Text**.

8. Open **Limited Text** and add some text, and then save the changes and close the document.

9. Open **Simple2** and create a text document named **Full Text** and contains some sample text.

10. Right-click **Simple1** and select **Sharing and Security**.

11. To enable file sharing, you need to select **If you understand the security risks but want to share files without running the wizard, click here** and then click Just enable file sharing. After that, you can check **Share this folder on the network** to configure the share, as shown in Figure 3-2, and click OK.

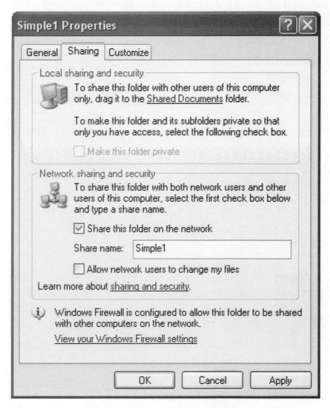

Figure 3-2: Sharing a folder

12. Right-click **Simple2** and then select **Sharing and Security**.

13. Select **Share this folder to the network** and **Allow network users to change my files**, and then click OK.

14. What differences in access security should you expect for Simple1 and Simple2?

_____

_____

_____

15. Do not exit **My Computer**.

■ Part B: Explore file access with Simple File Sharing enabled

Complete all project steps in this part on the computer running Windows Server 2003.

1. Select **File** and then **My Computer**.
2. Click Folders to open the **Folders** pane as the left-hand pane.
3. Expand **My Network Places**, **Entire Network**, **Microsoft Windows Network**, **Busicorp** and your Windows XP computer, and then select your Windows XP computer, as shown in Figure 3-3.

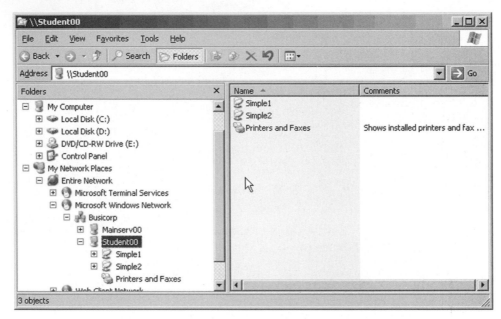

Figure 3-3: Shared folders

4. You should see **Simple1** and **Simple2** available.
5. Select **Simple1** in the left-hand pane and then double-click **Limited Text.txt** in the details pane to open the text file.
6. Type some additional text and select **File** and then **Save**. What happens and why?

_____

_____

7. Click OK. When the **Save As** dialog box appears, click Cancel.
8. Select **File** and then **Exit** and click No when prompted to save changes.
9. Right-click the details pane for **Simple1** and select **New** and then **Text Document**. What happens?

_____

_____

10. Click OK.

11. Select **Simple2** and then double-click **Full Text.txt** to open the text file.

12. Type some additional text and select **File** and then **Save**. What happens and why?

13. Right-click the details pane for **Simple2** and select **New** and then **Text Document**. What happens?

_____

_____

14. Do not exit **My Computer**.

■ Part C: Explore file sharing with Simple File Sharing disabled

Complete all project steps in this part on the computer running Windows XP Professional.

1. Open the **Tools** menu and select **Folder Options**.

2. Select the **View** tab and scroll to the bottom of the **View Properties** dialog box. Uncheck **Use simple file sharing (Recommended)**. Click OK.

3. Right-click **Simple1** and select **Sharing and Security**. The dialog box should look like the example shown in Figure 3-4.

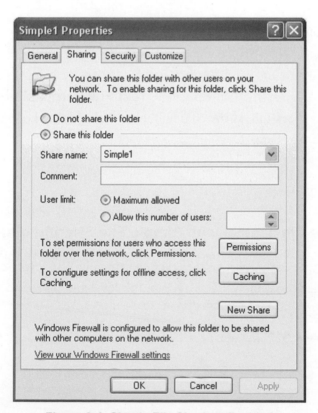

Figure 3-4: Simple File Sharing disabled

4. Click Permissions. What permissions are assigned?

_____

_____

5. Click Cancel and then OK to close the **Simple1 Properties** dialog box.
6. Right-click **Simple2** and select **Sharing and Security**.

7. Click Permissions. What permissions are assigned?

_____

_____

8. Check **Change** under **Deny**. What other permissions, if any, also change?

_____

_____

9. Click OK to close the **Permissions** dialog box. When the warning dialog box appears, click Yes to verify your action. The dialog box is warning you that denied rights take precedence over granted rights. In this case, all network users will be denied access to the folder's contents.
10. Click OK to close the **Simple2 Properties** dialog box.
11. Create a folder named **NewShare** at the root of the **C:** drive.
12. Right-click **NewShare** and run **Sharing and Security**.
13. Select **New Share** and assign the share name **Test Full Permissions**.
14. Click Permissions, check the **Allow** column for the **Full Control** permission, and click OK.
15. Click OK to create the share.
16. Exit **My Computer**.

■ Part D: Explore file access with Simple File Sharing disabled

Complete all project steps in this part on the computer running Windows Server 2003.

1. Select the computer running Windows XP in the left-hand pane and select **View** and then select **Refresh**. What shared folders do you see listed?

_____

_____

2. Select **Simple1** in the left-hand pane. What happens?

    _____

    _____

3. Open and edit **Limited Text.txt** and try to save the changes. Can you save the changes? Why or why not?

    _____

    _____

    _____

4. Close **Limited Text.txt**.
5. Select **Simple2** in the left-hand pane. What happens?

    _____

    _____

6. Right-click **Test Full Permissions** and run **Map Network Drive**. The **Map Network Drive** dialog box appears.
7. Click different user name.
8. Enter the following information:

    User name: *computername***Administrator**

    Password: **P*ssword**

    Replace *computername* with the name of the computer running Windows XP Professional.
9. Click OK.
10. Click Finish. A new window will open automatically for the mapped drive. Close the new window.
11. Click **My Computer** in the left-hand pane. The **My Computer** window should look similar to Figure 3-5.

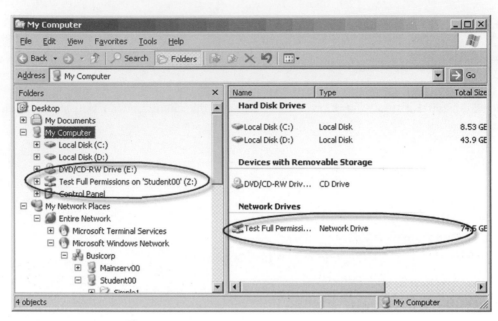

Figure 3-5: My Computer with mapped drive

12. Notice how the mapped network drive is identified.
13. Close **My Computer**.

Project 3.4	Promoting a Windows Server 2003 Computer to Domain Controller
Overview	You create an Active Directory domain by promoting the first domain server in that domain. This creates the domain directory structure. You promote a Windows Server 2003 computer to domain controller by configuring it for the domain controller role through the Manage Your Server utility. Once promoted, and unless demoted back to being a server and not a domain controller, the server can only be used as part of the domain. You can no longer log on to the server as a stand-alone server. Logging on to the server, you log on to the Active Directory domain. The domain management utilities are installed on the server during promotion. Also, any local users and groups are deleted. When promoting the first domain controller, the wizard checks for a Domain Name System (DNS) server that is authoritative for the domain. The DNS server maps host names to IP addresses in a TCP/IP network. An authoritative DNS server, one with the "official" mappings for the domain, is a requirement for an Active Directory domain. Because the network does not already have a DNS server, it will install DNS server support on the domain controller as part of the promotion process. During this project, you will promote your Windows Server 2003 computer to the domain controller role and create the Busicorp.com Active Directory domain.
Outcomes	After completing this project, you will know how to: ▲ promote Windows Server 2003 to the domain controller role ▲ create an Active Directory domain ▲ create domain users
What you'll need	To complete this project, you will need: ▲ a computer running Windows Server 2003 ▲ Windows Server 2003 installation software
Completion time	60 minutes (depending on computer configuration)
Precautions	If you are running this project as part of a larger classroom network, your instructor will provide alternate steps. Domain names must be unique, so your instructor will need to provide you with an alternate domain name. If you are performing this project on an existing network, you must review the project steps with your network administrator. Your network administrator may need to make changes or additions to the instructions and might specify a different domain name.

Depending on the network configuration in which you are working, your instructor or network administrator may specify a different domain name. Record that domain name below:

Alternate domain name: _____

If an alternate domain name is not provided, use the domain name specified in the project (Busicorp.com).

■ Part A: Promote a server to domain controller

Before a Windows Server 2003 computer can be used as a domain controller, it must be promoted to that role.

1. If the **Manage Your Server** dialog box is not open on your computer, open the **Start menu**, select **Administrative Tools**, and then select **Manage Your Server**.

2. Click **Add or remove a role**, as indicated in Figure 3-6.

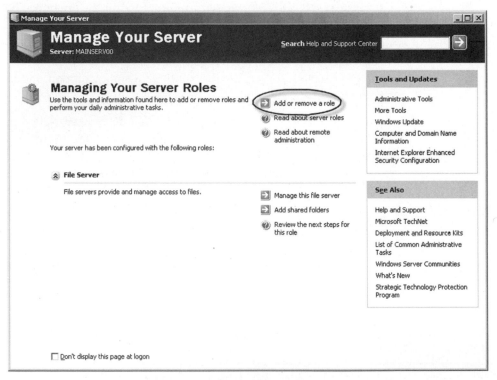

Figure 3-6: Add or remove a role

3. Review the preliminary steps and then click Next.

4. If prompted, choose **Custom Configuration** and click Next.

5. Select **Domain Controller** from the list of available roles and click Next.

6. Review the summary of selections and click Next.

7. The **Active Directory Installation Wizard** launches automatically. When the **Welcome** screen appears, click Next.

8. The **Operating System Compatibility** screen appears. Review the information about operating system compatibility and click Next.

9. The **Domain Controller Type** screen opens. Verify that **Domain controller for a new domain** is selected and click Next.

10. The **Create New Domain Screen** appears. Verify that **Domain in a new forest** is selected and click Next.

11. Select **No, just install and configure DNS on this computer** and click Next

12. The **New Domain Name** screen appears. Type **BUSICORP.COM** as the full DNS name for the new domain and click Next.

13. The **NetBIOS Domain Name** screen opens. Click Next to accept the default domain NetBIOS name.

14. The **Database and Log Folders** screen opens. Click Next to accept the default database and log folder locations.

15. The **Shared System Volume** screen appears. Click Next to accept the default SYSVOL folder location.

16. The **Permissions** screen opens. Leave the permissions at default, compatible with Windows 2000 or Windows Server 2003, and click Next.

17. The **Directory Services Restore Mode Administrator Password** screen appears. Type **P*ssword** in the Restore Mode Password and Confirm Password fields, and click Next.

18. The **Summary** screen opens. Review the selection summary and then click Next to start Active Directory installation. The wizard will create the Active Directory domain and configure the computer as the first domain controller. Insert the Windows Server 2003 installation CD when prompted. This process will take up to 20 minutes, depending on computer speed.

19. When the **Active Directory Installation Wizard** reports that installation is complete, click Finish.

20. When prompted, click Restart Now to restart the computer.

21. After restart, log on as **Administrator**. The **Configure Your Server Wizard** informs you that the computer is now a domain controller (Figure 3-8). Click **View the next steps for this role** and review the steps.

22. Close the **Help** box containing the configuration steps and then click Finish to close the **Configure Your Server Wizard**.

■ Part B: Create domain users and groups

Typically, one of the first steps after creating a new domain is creating domain users. You will create two domain users.

1. Open the **Start** menu, point to **All Programs**, select **Administrative Tools**, and then select **Active Directory Users and Computers**. This is the primary utility for managing your domain's logical structure and domain objects, including users.

2. Expand and then select your domain. What containers are listed?

_____

_____

3. Select **Computers** and verify that the container is empty.
4. Select **Domain Controllers** and verify that your Windows Server 2003 computer is listed as the only domain controller.
5. Click **Users**. Notice that the contents includes both users and groups.
6. Right-click your domain in the tree view pane (the left-hand pane), and select **New** and then **Organizational Unit**. This creates a new Organizational Unit (OU) that can be used as a container for domain objects.
7. Name the new OU **Project Stuff** and click OK.
8. Right-click **Project Stuff**, and select **New** and then **User**. You can create users in the Users container or in OUs that you have created.
9. Fill in the prompts as follows and then click Next:

   First name: **Standard**

   Initials: **(leave blank)**

   Last Name: **User**

   Full name: **(leave at default)**

   User logon name: **Standard**

   User logon name (pre-Windows 2000):   **Standard**

10. Type **P*ssword** as the password, uncheck **User must change password at next logon**, and click Next.
11. Click Finish.
12. Repeat steps 8 through 11 to create the following second user:

    First name: **Admin**

    Initials: **(leave blank)**

    Last Name: **User**

    Full name: **(leave at default)**

    User logon name: **MyAdmin**

    User logon name (pre-Windows 2000):   **MyAdmin**

13. Which name would you use to log on to a domain client? How do the two users you created differ?

_____

_____

_____

14. Right-click **Admin User** and select **Properties**.

15. Select the **Member Of** tab. What group(s) are listed?

_____

_____

16. Click Add.

17. Type **Administrators** and then click **Check Names**.

18. If the name verifies without any error, click OK. If there is an error, the most likely cause is that you misspelled the group name. What groups are listed now on the **Member Of** tab?

_____

_____

_____

19. Click OK to close the **Admin User Properties** dialog box.

20. Right-click **Project Stuff**, and select **New** and then **Group**.

21. Leave the group scope at default and type the name **MyGroup** in the **Group name** field.

22. Click OK to create the group.

23. Right-click **MyGroup** and select **Properties**.

24. Select the **Members** tab and click Add.

25. Type **Standard;MyAdmin**, as shown in Figure 3-7, and click Check Names.

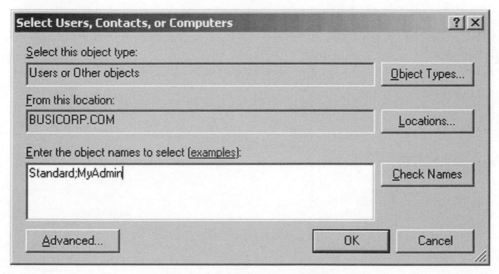

Figure 3-7: Adding group members

26. Click OK to add the members and then click OK to close the **Group Properties** dialog box.

27. Exit **Active Directory Users and Computers**.

■ **Part C: Create source folders**

You are creating folders to use as shared resources in the next project. You will create three folders at the root of drive C:. You will be making changes to folder security that may be unfamiliar to you. You will be modifying local access permissions for one of the folders. Local access permissions determine user access when the user is logged on locally to the computer on which the resource is located, but can also impact access permissions when accessing a folder through a share in an Active Directory network or in a peer-to-peer network when simple file sharing is not enabled.

1. Open the **Start** menu, select **My Computer**, and then navigate to the root of the **C:** drive.
2. Right-click in the details pane, and select **New** and then **Folder** to create a new folder. Create three new folders with the following names:

    LimitedSource

    FullSource

    NoSource
3. For each of the folders, complete the following steps:
    a. Open the folder.
    b. Right-click the details pane, and select **New** and then **Text Document**.
    c. Name the document *foldername***Text.txt**, for example, **LimitedSourceText.txt**.
    d. Open the text document and type a line of text.
    e. Save the changes and close the text document.
4. Right-click **FullSource** and select **Properties**.
5. Select the **Security** tab. The gray check boxes indicate security setting that the folder inherited from a point higher in the file hierarchy, in this case, from the drive root. The permissions shown in Figure 3-8 are the default permission settings.

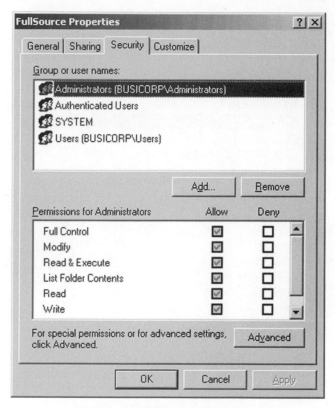

Figure 3-8: Default permissions

6. What permissions are allowed to the domain Users group?   What permissions are allowed
   to the Administrators group?

   _____

   _____

   _____

7. Click Add, type **MyGroup**, click Check Names, and then click OK. You should see
   MyGroup in the name list.

8. If not already selected, select **MyGroup**. What permissions are granted by default?

   _____

   _____

9. Notice that the check boxes are not gray for this group. That is because the permissions are
   not inherited. Instead, you are explicitly assigning the permissions to **MyGroup**.

10. Check **Full Control** in the **Allow** column. Your permissions should look like the example
    shown in Figure 3-9.

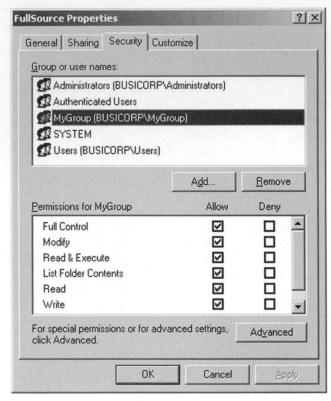

Figure 3-9: Explicit permission assignment

11. Click OK.

12. Right-click **NoSource** and select **Permissions**. Add **My Group** to the permissions list and check **Full Control** in the **Deny** column.

13. Click OK. When prompted to verify your action, click Yes.

14. Exit **My Computer**.

Project 3.5	Adding an Active Directory Client
Overview	You configure Active Directory clients, and servers, for that matter, by having them join as domain members. After joining a domain, you can then use a domain user account to log on to the domain and access domain resources. You can also manage users and computers that belong to the domain.
	You continue setting up your Active Directory domain during this project. You will first make sure that you've ensured that your client will be kept up-to-date and then you add the computer as a domain member. To test, you'll log on with a domain user account.
Outcomes	After completing this project, you will know how to: ▲ configure automatic updates

	▲ join a computer to a domain
	▲ log on to a domain
What you'll need	To complete this project, you will need:
	▲ complete Project 3.4
	▲ client computer running Windows XP Professional
	▲ Internet access (for "Enabling automatic updates")
Completion time	30 minutes
Precautions	The instructions in this project assume you have a two-node network with one computer running Windows XP Professional and one computer running Windows Server 2003. If the computers you are working with are part of a larger classroom network, review the project steps with your instructor or network administrator, because changes or additions to the installation instructions may be required.

■ Part A: Enable automatic updates

Security is often of critical concern in an Active Directory environment. In fact, it is often a major factor in domain design. Before joining the domain, you will use the following steps to update your computer and configure automatic updates to ensure that security patches are applied automatically as they become available.

If your computer does not have Internet access, skip these steps and continue with the steps under Part C.

1. Open the **Start** menu, point to **All Programs**, and select **Windows Update.**

2. If prompted, follow the on-screen install of the Microsoft Update ActiveX control. This control is required.

3. When prompted with the **Welcome to Microsoft Update** screen shown in Figure 3-10, click Turn on Automatic Updates.

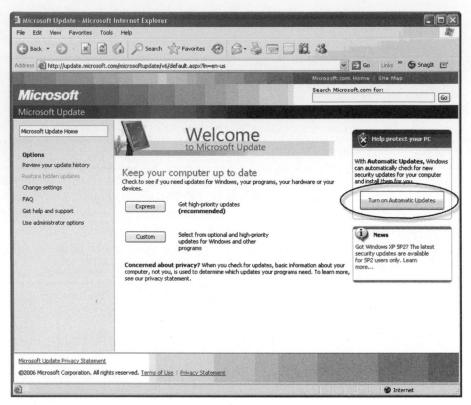

Figure 3-10: Automatic Updates

4. Click OK to accept the default automatic updates schedule.

5. Click Express to identify the high-priority updates needed by your computer.

6. When prompted, click Download and Install Now to install the current updates.

   This process can take several minutes, up to an hour, depending on computer speed, connection speed, and the number of required updates.

7. If prompted, click Restart Now to restart the computer.

8. After the computer restarts, log on as **Administrator**.

■ Part B: Prepare to join a domain

You will need access to the DNS server responsible for the domain to complete these steps. If you do not know the IP address for your Windows Server 2003 computer, open a command prompt on the computer and run IPconfig. Record the address below for your reference:

   IP Address: _____

1. Open the **Control Panel** and launch **Network Connections**.

2. Right-click your local connection **(Local Area Connection)** and run **Properties**.

3. Select **Internet Protocol (TCP/IP)** and click Properties.

4. If not already selected, select **Use the following DNS server addresses** and enter the IP address for your domain controller as the primary DNS server. The properties should look similar to those shown in Figure 3-11.

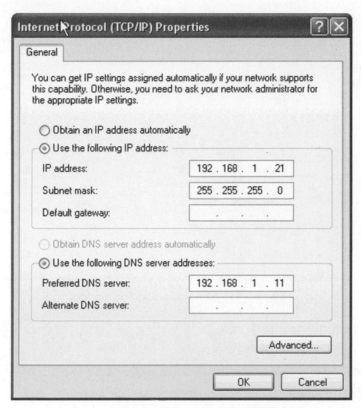

Figure 3-11: Configuring a primary DNS server

5. Click OK to save the property changes and then click Close to exit the connection properties.

6. You can use a TCP/IP utility ping to verify. Open the **Start** menu, point to **All Programs**, point to **Accessories**, and select **Command Prompt** to open a command prompt window.

7. Execute the following: **ping *servername***. Replace *servername* with your Windows Server 2003 computer's name, for example, mainserv00.

8. Close the **Command Prompt** window.

9. In the **Network Connections** window, click the Up navigation command icon in the toolbar (see Figure 3-12) to return to the **Control Panel**.

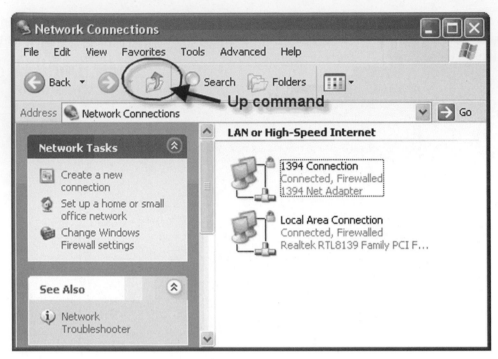

Figure 3-12: Toolbar navigation control

10. Double-click **Administrative Tools**.

11. Double-click **Computer Management**.

12. Under **System Tools**, expand **Local Users and Groups** and select **Groups**.

13. Right-click **Administrators** and select **Properties**. What users, if any, currently belong to this group?

14. Click Cancel and then exit **Computer Management**.

■ Part C: Join a domain

1. In the **Administrative Tools** window, click Up (in the toolbar) to return to the **Control Panel**.

2. In the **Control Panel**, double-click **System** and then select the **Computer Name** tab in the **Systems Properties** dialog box, as shown in Figure 3-13.

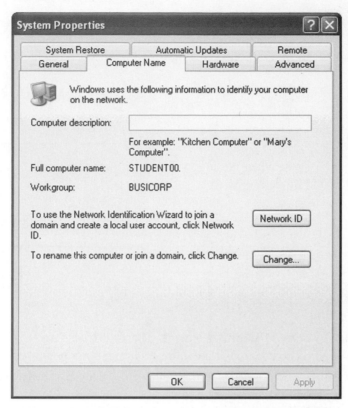

Figure 3-13: Computer name (as workgroup member)

3. Click Change.

4. Select **Domain** under **Member of** and type **BUSICORP.COM** as the domain name.

5. Click OK.

6. When prompted, type **Administrator** as the user name and the Administrator's password, and then click OK. When you promoted your server to domain controller, the local administrator was promoted to a domain administrator, but the password did not change.

7. A dialog box informs you that you have successfully joined the domain. Click OK to close the dialog box.

8. A dialog box informs you that you must restart the computer for the changes to take effect. Click OK to close the dialog box.

9. Click OK in the **System Properties** dialog box to close the dialog box.

10. A dialog box prompts you to restart your computer. Close any open windows or running applications and then click Yes in this dialog box to restart your computer.

■ **Part C: Verify membership changes**

1. Allow your computer to finish restart. How has the initial screen changed?

   _____

   _____

   _____

2. Press Ctrl + Alt + Del and when the logon dialog box appears, click Options. What is listed in the **Log on to** field by default?

   _____

   _____

   _____

3. Select **BUSICORP** from the **Log on to** drop-down list.

4. Log on as **MyAdmin**.

5. After logging on, launch the **Control Panel**. The **Control Panel** is in **Category View** because Windows XP is configured at the default settings for a new user.

6. Select **Performance and Maintenance** and then select **System** to open the **System Properties** dialog box.

7. Select the **Computer Name** tab. How has the full computer name changed?

   _____

   _____

8. Exit the **System Properties** dialog box and select **Administrative Tools**.

9. Launch **Computer Management**.

10. Under **System Tools**, expand **Local Users and Groups** and select **Groups**.

11. Right-click **Administrators** and select **Properties**. What users, if any, currently belong to this group? From the standpoint of security, what does this mean?

    _____

    _____

    _____

12. Close the **Group Properties** dialog box and exit **Computer Management**.

13. Exit **Control Panel**.

Project 3.6	Exploring an Active Directory Network
Overview	The procedures for resource sharing in an Active Directory domain are very similar to those for sharing resources from a Windows XP Professional computer with Simple File Sharing disabled. You can specify the share name, maximum number of users, and permissions. You can also configure the shared folder so it can be cached, so that the client computer can keep a local copy of the folder and its contents, but any discussion of caching is beyond the scope of this project.
	The procedures for accessing shared resources and mapping a local drive letter to a shared folder are also the same. The differences come primarily in how security is managed. Security is centrally managed in an Active Directory domain and is based on your domain user account. Permissions are based on those assigned to your user account and to any groups to which your account belongs. When determining your effective security, what you can actually do with the resource, both local and share permissions are considered. If access is explicitly denied to the user or a group to which the user belongs, as shared permissions or local permissions, the denied permissions override allowed permissions. There is one exception, in which an explicit allow can override an inherited deny.
	As you might guess, permission assignments in an Active Directory domain can become quite complex if you aren't careful. One key to effective domain management is keeping permission assignments as simple as possible. For example, whenever possible, you should assign permissions at the group level rather than the user level and limit explicit user permission assignments to special case exceptions.
Outcomes	After completing this project, you will know how to: ▲ share folder resources ▲ access shared resources
What you'll need	To complete this project, you will need: ▲ to complete Projects 3.4 and 3.5 ▲ your Windows XP and Windows Server 2003 computers
Completion time	60 minutes (approximate, depending on computer configuration and speed)
Precautions	If you are performing the project as part of a larger classroom network, your instructor may provide alternate steps.
	If you are performing this project on an existing network, you must review the project steps with your network administrator. Your network administrator may need to make changes or additions to the project steps.

■ Part A: Review client membership

You will complete these project steps on your domain controller. You should be logged on as Administrator to your domain controller.

1. Open the **Start** menu, point to **Administrative Tools**, and then select **Active Directory Users and Computers**. If necessary, expand your domain.

2. Select **Computers**. You should see your client computer listed, as shown in Figure 3-14.

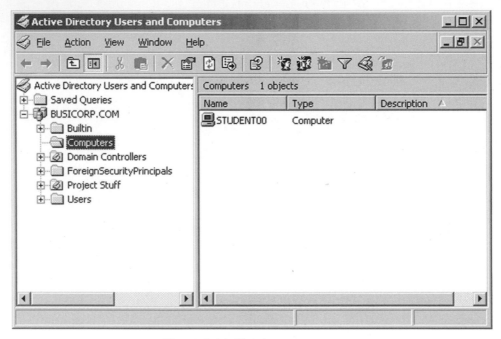

Figure 3-14: Member computer

3. When was your Windows XP computer added to the **Computers** container?

_____

_____

4. Right-click your client computer and select **Properties**. What is given as the computer's role?

_____

_____

5. Select the **Operating System** tab. What is the operating system and service pack level? How could you change this information about the computer?

_____

_____

6. Review the properties on the remaining tabs. Why don't the computer properties list any information about the computer user?

_____

_____

7. Select **Project Stuff** and verify that the users and group you created in Project 3.4 are listed.

8. Close the **Computer Properties** dialog box and exit **Active Directory Users and Computers**.

■ Part B: Share resources

You will complete these project steps on your domain controller. You should be logged on as **Administrator** to your domain controller.

1. Launch **My Computer** and navigate to the root of the **C:** drive.

2. Right-click FullSource and select **Sharing and Security**. Select the **Share this folder** option button.

3. Click Permissions.

4. Click Add, type **MyGroup**, click Check Names, and then click OK.

5. Under **Allow**, check **Full Control**, as shown in Figure 3-15.

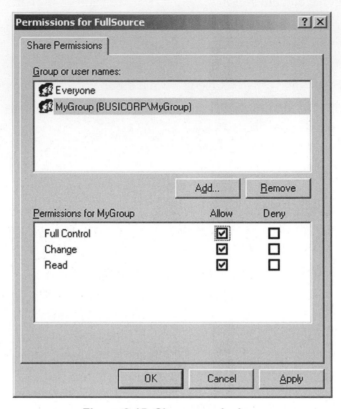

Figure 3-15: Share permissions

6. Why should you assign the permissions to the group instead of the group members?

   _____

   _____

7. Click OK to save the permissions settings.
8. Click OK to share the folder.
9. Repeat steps 2 through 8 to share **NoSource** with the same share permissions.
10. Repeat steps 2 through 8 to share **LimitedSource** with the following change: Allow the **Read** permission only for **MyGroup**.

■ Part C: Access resources

Complete these project steps on the computer running Windows XP Professional. You should be logged on as the user account Standard.

1. Launch **My Computer** and click **Folders** to display the folder tree view in the left-hand pane.

2. Expand **My Network Places**, **Entire Network**, **Microsoft Windows Network**, **Busicorp**, and your domain controller. Select your domain controller.

3. Attempt the following with each of the shared resources during this project (**FullSource**, **LimitedSource**, and **NoSource**):

   a. Select the folder in the tree view to view the folder contents.

   b. Open the sample text document.

   c. Edit and save the sample text document.

   d. Create a new text file.

   e. Map a network drive for the shared folder. To map a network drive, right-click the folder, select **Map Network Drive**, and click Finish to accept the default drive ID.

Record your results in Table 3-1. Enter Successful for any action you could complete. For any action you were not able to complete, explain what happened.

Table 3-1: Access results

	FullSource	Limited Source	NoSource
Access folder			
Open text file			
Modify text file			
Add new text file			
Map network drive			

4. The share permissions for **NoShare** allowed **Full Control** for **MyGroup**. Why did you get the results that you saw? **Tip**: Check the folder's local and share security on the domain controller.

5. Close **My Computer**.

4

NETWORK TOPOLOGIES

PROJECTS

Project 4.1	Understanding Key Concepts
Overview	Part of each network's design is its topology. It's important to understand the role of topology, as well as wired and wireless topologies, you might encounter. This also includes terms related to OSI layer 2 communication technologies.
	Because term definitions can sometimes vary on the context in which they are used, it is important to be able to recognize terms and how they are used in the context of network topologies.
Outcomes	After completing this project, you will know how to:
	▲ identify key terms and concepts related to networking topologies
What you'll need	To complete this project, you will need:
	▲ the worksheet below
Completion time	20 minutes
Precautions	None

The worksheet includes a list of networking terms on the left and descriptions on the right. Match each term with the description that it most closely matches. You will *not* use all descriptions. Each description can be used only once.

___ 10Base2

A. Network device that can be used to connect two cable segments as a single network segment

___ 10BaseT

B. Physical topology in which all devices connect to one central point

___ Coax

C. Access method in which access is managed by means of a rotating token

___ Bus

D. Star topology Ethernet network wired with twisted pair cable

___ Ring

E. Bus topology transmission error that occurs when two or more computers try to transmit at the same time

___ Star

F. Network device that amplifies the network signal to extend network range

___ Collision

G. The physical topology used when implementing a 10Base2 network

___ FDDI	H. Network device used to join network segments
___ IEEE 802.5	I. Cable with a central conductive core surrounded by a dielectric, shield, and insulator
___ IEEE 802.11g	J. Central connection device for a Token Ring network wired as a physical star
___ MAU	K. Bus topology Ethernet network using Thicknet cable
___ Hub	L. Bus topology Ethernet network using Thinnet cable
___ Repeater	M. Fiber optic dual-ring networking scheme
___ Bridge	N. Physical topology in which devices connect in a circular loop
___ Router	O. Current wireless networking standard
	P. Central connection device for an Ethernet network wired as a physical star

Project 4.2	Recognizing Physical Topologies
Overview	An important part of any network design is the network topology. In modern networks, the network topology can be either a wired or wireless topology. The physical topology can usually be determined through simple observation, by looking at the cable and connection devices used.
	As part of documenting a network, you need to be able to draw simple network topologies and to recognize network sketches. During this project you are presented with a series of sketches and you need to identify the topology.
Outcomes	After completing this project, you will know how to:
	▲ recognize physical network topology
What you'll need	To complete this project, you will need:
	▲ the worksheet below
Completion time	10 minutes
Precautions	None

For each of the following figures, identify the topology as bus, ring, star, mesh, or ad hoc. You will use each network type.

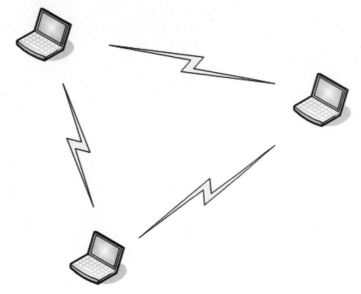

Figure 4-1

1. **Ad hoc**_____

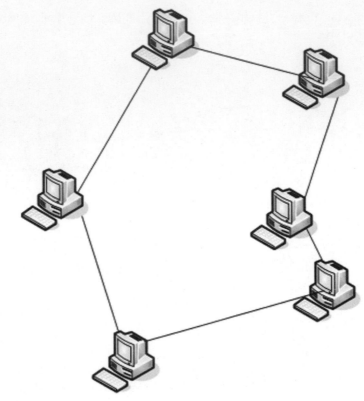

Figure 4-2

2. **Ring**_____

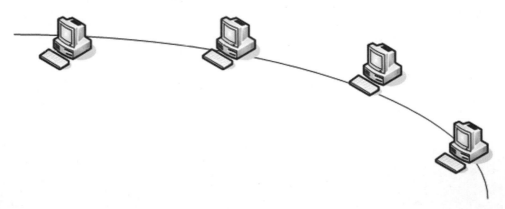

Figure 4-3

3. **Bus**_____

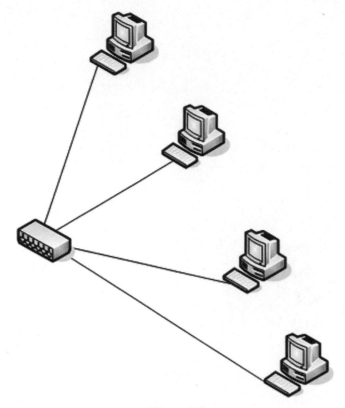

Figure 4-4

4. **Star**_____

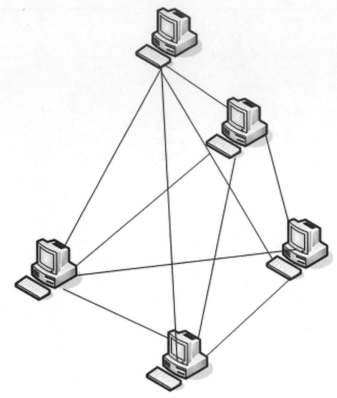

Figure 4-5

5. **Mesh**_____

Project 4.3	Recognizing Logical Topologies
Overview	Logical topologies can be more difficult to identify than physical topologies. A logical topology looks like one type of topology but works like another. In most cases, the network is wired as a physical star, but operates as either a logical bus or a logical ring.
	The two most common logical networks are Ethernet and Token Ring networks that are wired as a physical star. There are similarities in both cases. The star is formed using central connection devices. Connections to the computers are made using twisted pair cable. The difference between them is that each network is functionally equivalent to bus (for Ethernet) or ring (for Token Ring), with different connection hardware used in each case.
Outcomes	After completing this project, you will know how to:
	▲ identify features of a logical ring
	▲ identify features of a logical bus

What you'll need	To complete this project, you will need:
	▲ the worksheet below
Completion time	20 minutes
Precautions	None

Place each of the following statements in the appropriate column in Table 4-1. You will use all statements. You may use a statement more than once.

Wired as a physical star.

Performance may suffer due to collisions.

Determinant access method.

Uses MAUs to connect computers.

Uses Hubs to connect computers.

Data travels linearly from source to all computers.

Most common logical topology.

Does not suffer from collisions.

Device must wait for open token to transmit.

All computers have equal access to the network.

Most often seen in legacy networks.

Failing node does not cause the entire network to fail.

Devices can be added without interrupting the network.

Table 4-1: Logical topologies

Logical Ring	Logical Bus

Project 4.4	Designing a Network
Overview	While it is important that you understand network topology options, you also need to know how to apply this knowledge in practical situations. This means that you need to understand how available topologies relate to network design and deployment options, as well the requirements for deploying a network based on a specific topology. During this project you will answer questions about network design based on a short case study describing network requirements.
Outcomes	After completing this project, you will know how to: ▲ identify the most appropriate network topology selection(s) ▲ identify requirements for deploying a network topology
What you'll need	To complete this project, you will need: ▲ the following worksheet
Completion time	30 minutes
Precautions	None

The Busicorp network is currently made up of two unconnected network segments. One segment is wired as a physical bus topology using 10Base2 and the other is wired as a logical Token Ring network. The company has leased additional office space on the same floor as its current offices and is expanding, adding 40 additional computers. You need to design the wired network topology for the new network segment and identify options for connecting the existing network segments.

1. What should you use as the physical topology for the new network segment?

   _____
   _____
   _____

2. What should you use as the logical topology?

   _____
   _____
   _____

3. What hardware will be needed in the computers to connect to the new network segment?

   _____
   _____
   _____

4. What connection equipment, if any, will be needed on the network to connect the computers?

   _____
   _____
   _____

5. What would be needed to connect the new network segments to each of the old network segments and allow them to communicate as one logical network for routing purposes?

    _____
    _____
    _____

6. What would be needed to have each network segment treated as a separate network for routing purposes?

    _____
    _____
    _____

7. What would you have to do if you wanted each of the old network segments to use the same network design as the new segment?

    _____
    _____
    _____

8. How could you justify upgrading the physical bus network?

    _____
    _____
    _____

9. How could you justify upgrading the logical Token Ring network?

    _____
    _____
    _____

10. What could you do if you want to avoid running cable for the new network, but have the new computers be able to communicate with each other and with the existing computers?

    _____
    _____
    _____

Project 4.5	Network Inventory
Overview	Before you can support and maintain a network, you need to know how it is structured. In other words, you need to understand the physical and logical topology used. The physical topology can be determined through simple observation, by looking at how the network is wired. The logical topology can sometimes be determined through observation, but more often requires additional research.
	The process of checking the network to see how it is structured and how computers connect to the network is sometimes referred to as taking the network inventory. You will take an inventory of your network during this project and document the network design.
Outcomes	After completing this project, you will know how to: ▲ determine the physical topology in use ▲ determine the logical topology in use
What you'll need	To complete this project, you will need: ▲ access to your network and connection devices ▲ client computer running Windows XP Professional
Completion time	45 minutes (approximate, depending on computer configuration and speed)
Precautions	If you are performing this project on an existing network, you must review the project steps with your network administrator. Your network administrator may need to make changes or additions to the instructions.

Take an inventory of your network and answer the questions that follow:

1. What is the network's physical topology?

   _____

   _____

   _____

2. What connection devices, if any, are used on the network?

   _____

   _____

   _____

3. Describe how your Windows XP computer is physically connected to the network.

   _____

   _____

   _____

4. Physically disconnect your Windows XP computer from the network. If you have a built-in wireless adapter, disable the adapter. How does this impact the other computers on the network?

   _____
   _____
   _____

5. What symptoms, if any, do you observe at your Windows XP computer?

   _____
   _____
   _____

6. Reconnect your Windows XP computer to the network.

7. Open the **Control Panel**. If **the Control Panel** is configured in **Category View**, switch to **Classic View**.

8. Open **Network Connections** and double-click **Local Area Connection** (or double-click **Wireless Connection** if you have a wireless adapter). You should see a dialog box similar to Figure 4-6.

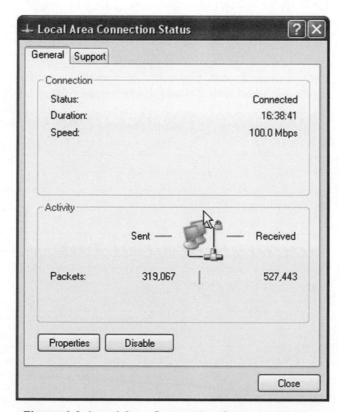

Figure 4-6: Local Area Connection Status dialog box

9. Click Properties to display a dialog box similar to the one shown in Figure 4-7.

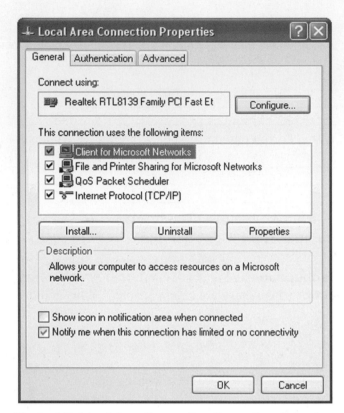

Figure 4-7: Local Area Connection Properties dialog box

10. What is the network adapter listed in the **Connect using** field?

_____

_____

_____

11. How can you tell the logical topology typc?

_____

_____

_____

12. What logical topology is your network using?

_____

_____

_____

13. Click Configure under **Connect using**. Review the configuration settings and then click OK.

14. Close the **Local Area Connection Status** dialog box.

15. Close any open windows.

5
NETWORK MEDIA AND DEVICES

PROJECTS

Project 5.1	Understanding Key Concepts
Overview	Media and hardware selections are critical decisions during network design and critical choices during network implementation. You need to make selections that not only meet current needs but also, as much as possible, continue to support the network as it grows and as technology changes. Some choices, like whether to use twisted pair or coaxial cable, are obvious. Others, like the specific category of cable to use, require more thought. Because term definitions can sometimes vary depending on the context in which they are used, it is important to be able to recognize terms and how they are used in the context of network media and devices.
Outcomes	After completing this project, you will know how to: ▲ identify key terms and concepts related to network media and devices
What you'll need	To complete this project, you will need: ▲ the worksheet below
Completion time	20 minutes
Precautions	None

The worksheet includes a list of networking terms on the left and descriptions on the right. Match each term with the description that it most closely matches. You will *not* use all descriptions. Each description can be used only once.

___	Bridging loop	A. Measurement of opposition to varying electrical current
___	Radio grade	B. Type of cable used in Thinnet and Thicknet network applications
___	STP	C. Interference affecting electronic signals and caused by a strong magnetic field
___	UTP	D. Area within an Ethernet network in which all devices compete for access to the same logical or physical cable segment
___	Coax	E. Specification for coaxial cable rated for network applications
___	Broadcast domain	F. Multiport bridge connection device operating at OSI layer 2

___	Collision domain	G. Type of cable used to connect devices in a 10BaseT network
___	Hub	H. Unit of measurement for resistance or impedance
___	Switch	I. Physical star connection device that connects all attached devices in the same collision domain
___	EMI	J. Teflon-based, fire-resistant cable installation used with cable run through walls and cable races
___	Impedance	K. Set of nodes configured to receive broadcasts as a group
___	Induction	L. Condition where packets are passed between devices without ever reaching the destination segment.
___	Plenum	M. Cable containing multiple pairs of wires that are twisted periodically and covered with a foil or braid shield
___	Ohm	N. Process by which a moving electrical current causes a voltage on a nearby wire
		O. Plastic commonly used for cable insulation that can release toxic fumes when burned
		P. Thicknet cable tap

Project 5.2	Comparing Physical Media Applications
Overview	Different types of copper-wire cables are designed for use in different network applications. You need to be able to match up the cable type with the network application so that you can make appropriate design decisions when designing your network. This means that you should be able to identify a cable type by both its physical description and a description of how it is used. This is complicated by the fact that some descriptions overlap, applying to more than one basic cable type.

	In this project you will be matching cable types to cable design and application descriptions. For now, you are concerned only about the basic cable type, not its specific category characteristics.
Outcomes	After completing this project, you will know how to: ▲ recognize a cable type by a description of its physical structure ▲ recognize a cable type based on how it is used
What you'll need	To complete this project, you will need: ▲ the worksheet below
Completion time	20 minutes
Precautions	None

The worksheet includes a table (Table 5-1) with different basic cable types and a list of statements that describe one or more of them. Check the boxes for the letters that best describe each cable type. Each statement applies to at least one type of cable. Some statements may apply to multiple cable types.

A. Has a single conductor.

B. Has multiple conductors.

C. Has a foil or braid shield to minimize EMI.

D. Used to wire physical star networks.

E. Used to wire physical bus networks.

F. Used in Ethernet logical bus applications.

G. Used in Token Ring logical bus applications.

H. Can be used with an IBM hermaphroditic connector.

I. Can be used with an RJ-45 connector.

J. Can be used with a vampire tap.

Table 5-1: Cable types

Network cable type	A	B	C	D	E	F	G	H	I	J
UTP										
STP										
Coax										

Project 5.3	Identifying Physical Media Types
Overview	Each basic cable type includes multiple types or categories of cable, each with its own unique characteristics and physical applications. You not only need to know what kind of cable you need to use in a network application, either coax, STP, or UTP, but also need to select the appropriate type or category of cable. You also need to understand the type of connectors required for each. When selecting cable for a networking project, you need to ensure that the cable will support the current network application and communication bandwidth. Whenever possible, you want to choose cable that will continue to meet your needs as the network expands and as network bandwidths increase. This project addresses each of the basic cable types separately so that you can identify the uses of coax, STP, and UTP cable types, without concerning yourself with the possible overlap between the cable types. You will also identify common connector types.
Outcomes	After completing this project, you will know how to: ▲ identify coaxial cable types by application ▲ identify STP cable types by features and applications ▲ identify UTP cable categories by features and applications ▲ identify commonly used connectors
What you'll need	To complete this project, you will need: ▲ the worksheet below ▲ cable samples to examine, if possible
Completion time	30 minutes
Precautions	None

■ Part A: Coaxial cable grades

Match each coaxial cable grade with the best description of its characteristics and applications for which it is used. You will use each description only once. You will use all of the descriptions.

____   RG-6

A. 75-ohm cable used for cable TV only and having up to four layers of shielding

____   RG-8

B. Stranded-core thin Ethernet cable used for military applications only

___ RG-11	C. Solid-core thin Ethernet cable
___ RG-58/U	D. Used to connect IBM 3270 system to terminals
___ RG-58 A/U	E. 75-ohm cable used for ARCNET and cable TV, recognizable by its large outer housing
___ RG-58 C/U	F. 93-ohm cable used for cable TV transmission applications only
___ RG-59	G. Stranded-core thin Ethernet cable used for civilian network applications
___ RG-62	H. Used for thick Ethernet applications and requires a vampire tap and drop cable to connect to network devices

■ Part B: STP cable types

Match each STP cable type with the best description of its characteristics and applications for which it is used. You will use each description only once. You will use all of the descriptions.

___ Type 1	A. Two pairs of 26-gauge flat copper wire designed for routing under carpets, but limited by its tendency for signal loss over distance
___ Type 2	B. Two pairs of 22-gauge copper wire used to connect nodes to the MAU in an IBM Token Ring network
___ Type 6	C. Two pairs of 26-gauge copper wire with a solid or stranded core and plenum jacket, typically used in backbone implementations between floors
___ Type 8	D. Four pairs of 22-gauge copper wire used as a hybrid cable supporting multiple concurrent applications, such as voice and data
___ Type 9	E. Two pairs of 26-gauge copper that can be used as a patch cable or to connect nodes to a MAU

■ Part C: UTP cable categories

Match each UTP cable category with the best description of its characteristics and applications for which it is used. You will use each description only once. You will use all of the descriptions.

___ Cat 1

A. Used in legacy 4-Mbps Token Ring networks, but no longer recognized under the 568-A standard

___ Cat 2

B. Certified to 100 Mbps for use in Ethernet networks, but sometimes found in higher bandwidth networks, even though not certified for those applications

___ Cat 3

C. Used in 16-Mbps Token Ring networks only

___ Cat 4

D. Certified up to 10 Gbps for Ethernet, 625 MHz for transmission, and specified as the standard cable for 10GBaseT networks

___ Cat 5

E. Certified for no higher than 1000 Mbps (1 Gbps) and found in a large number of physical star Ethernet networks

___ Cat 5e

F. Found in legacy 10BaseT networks and certified at no more than 10 Mbps

___ Cat 6

G. Voice-grade cable not suitable for data transmission applications

___ Cat 6e

H. Certified for up to 1.2 GHz, depending on the application and used for full-motion video and special government manufacturing applications, but has no current LAN applications

___ Cat 7

I. Certified for up to 10 Gbps for Ethernet applications and up to 400-MHz transmissions

■ Part D: Common connectors

Write in the name of the connector below each of the following figures. The connectors shown are for various cable types, including coaxial, UTP, STP, and fiber optic.

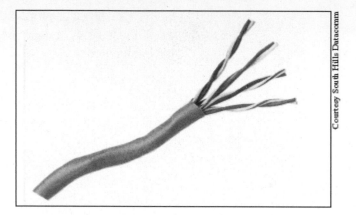

Figure 5-1

1. _____

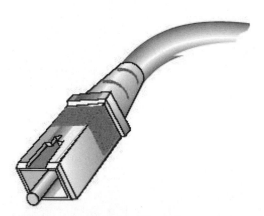

Figure 5-2

2. _____

Figure 5-3

3. _____

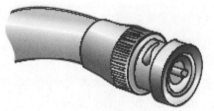

Figure 5-4

4. _____

Project 5.4	Comparing Network Scenarios
Overview	Not only do you need to understand the characteristics of different types of network media, you need to be able to apply this knowledge to meet practical, real-world networking requirements. This means balancing several factors, such as the physical environment, equipment costs, existing networks (if any), computer operating systems and hardware, and communication requirements. The final solution is often a compromise based on networking requirements, budgetary restrictions, and even network administrator or IT personnel preferences.
	When designing a network, you make your best choices based on requirements, restrictions, and the existing environment. You need to remain flexible after developing your design because sometimes issues arise during implementation that were not obvious during the design phase. This can make it necessary for you to make last-minute changes. However, these need to be avoided whenever possible because changes tend to be more expensive and more complicated the later you make them in the process. Because of this, you need to consider not only the technologies that you plan to use, but also other available technologies.
	In this project, you will look at three different network scenarios in which a company is moving into a new office space. In each scenario, there is a physical environment and different network requirements.
Outcomes	After completing this project, you will know how to:
	▲ identify the appropriate media selections for a given network scenario
	▲ identify additional hardware requirements
	▲ discuss features, benefits, and drawbacks of a specific media type
What you'll need	To complete this project, you will need:
	▲ the following worksheet
Completion time	45 minutes
Precautions	None

■ Part A: Generic network

A company is moving into a new office space. The space has an open floor plan. The office partitions are designed to facilitate routing physical network cables. The network budget allows for the purchase of new cabling and connection hardware, including network adapters, as necessary. However, you have been directed to keep costs as low as possible. The company wants to install a network with a minimum bandwidth of at least 100 Mbps. The plan should allow for future expansion and for eventually taking the bandwidth to 1 Gbps. The final network should not have any routing requirements.

1. Compare the appropriateness of each of the following media types for this scenario:

   a. STP

   _____

   _____

   b. UTP

   _____

   _____

   c. Coax

   _____

   _____

   d. Fiber optic

   _____

   _____

   e. Wireless

   _____

   _____

2. Which media type should you use to wire the network (be as specific as possible)? Why?

   _____

   _____

3. Describe the general network configuration.

   _____

   _____

4. What types of connection hardware, including cable connectors, would you use to connect network devices?

   _____

   _____

5. What guidelines should you follow for wiring the network?

   _____

   _____

6. What would be necessary to upgrade the network to 1 Gbps, based on your initial design?

_____

_____

■ Part B: Wiring concerns

A company is moving into new office space. There is a small room off the main part of the office that will be used as a secure server room. The servers will be wired using cables and a 100-Mbps switch brought over from the current office. Unfortunately, there is no way to route cable from this room to the rest of the office, nor is there any place to route network cables without running them across a concrete floor. The project budget includes funds to purchase new network and connection hardware, as necessary. Reliable connectivity is a higher concern than available bandwidth.

1. Compare the appropriateness of each of the following media types for this scenario:
   a. STP

_____

_____

   b. UTP

_____

_____

   c. Coax

_____

_____

   d. Fiber optic

_____

_____

   e. Wireless

_____

_____

2. Except for the servers in the secure server room, which media type should you use to wire the network (be as specific as possible)? Why?

   _____

   _____

3. What types of connection hardware, including cable connectors, would you use to connect network devices?

   _____

   _____

4. Describe how you would connect the servers to the rest of the network.

   _____

   _____

5. What are potential concerns with this network configuration?

   _____

   _____

6. What actions can you take to avoid potential problems?

   _____

   _____

7. Which network device(s), if any, could be a bottleneck and potential point of failure bringing down the network?

   _____

   _____

■ Part C: Noise concerns

A company is moving into a new shared office and manufacturing space. Most users work on the manufacturing floor. The manufacturing equipment emits high levels of both magnetic and radio frequency interference. The space is designed to physically protect network cables from damage when properly routed, but some cables will be routed next to or under manufacturing equipment. The in-house IT staff is responsible for network and computer equipment maintenance. The network should use the same topology and media throughout to minimize the number and variety of spares that must be kept on hand.

1. Compare the appropriateness of each of the following media types for this scenario:

   a. STP

   _____

   _____

   b. UTP

   _____

   _____

   c. Coax

   _____

   _____

   d. Fiber optic

   _____

   _____

   e. Wireless

   _____

   _____

2. What is the primary concern in the ambient environment as it relates to network design and implementation?

   _____

   _____

3. Which media type should you use to wire the network (be as specific as possible)? Why?

   _____

   _____

4. What types of connection hardware, including cable connectors, would you use to connect network devices?

   _____

   _____

5. From the standpoint of cost, how does this network design compare to other common network configurations?

_____

_____

Project 5.5	Choosing the Right Device
Overview	Media is only part of the design decision when setting up a new network or expanding (or upgrading) an existing network. You must also select appropriate network devices, as needed, to meet communication, reliability, and configuration requirements. This project has you choose network devices based on network configuration and support requirements.
Outcomes	After completing this project, you will know how to: ▲ choose appropriate network devices to meet network requirements
What you'll need	To complete this project, you will need: ▲ the following worksheet
Completion time	40 minutes
Precautions	None

For each of the following network requirement descriptions, choose the network device or devices that meet your support needs and answer the questions about your selections.

1. You have two unconnected network segments, one Token Ring and other Ethernet, both wired as physical stars. They should be treated as a single network connection after they are connected, but traffic local to a physical segment should be kept local to that segment.

    a. What kind of device should you use to connect the segments?

    _____

    _____

    b. How is traffic filtered?

    _____

    _____

    c. What are possible performance concerns with traffic moving between the segments?

    _____

    _____

2. Some employees have both computers and dumb terminals on their desks. Some employees have to share terminals, making for constant interruptions. The dumb terminals are required for accessing information from a mainframe computer. Applications and data are gradually being migrated from the mainframe to PC servers, but this process will take at least two more years to complete. You want to get rid of the terminals.

    a. What kind of device would let you get rid of the terminals and connect the computers to the mainframe?

    _____

    _____

    b. At what layer or layers of the OSI model does this type of device operate?

    _____

    _____

    c. What are the possible terminology concerns when discussing this configuration with others?

    _____

    _____

3. A network is wired as a physical bus. You are extending the cable to include another area of the office and add computers to the network. When you connect the additional cable, even before connecting any new computers, users start complaining about intermittent network problems. You cannot reliably reproduce any of the problems.

    a. What kind of device do you need to correct this problem?

    _____

    _____

    b. How would you rewire the network to correct the problem?

    _____

    _____

    c. What is the possible signal-quality concern with this configuration?

    _____

    _____

    d.   What is the maximum number of devices of this type can you include on a single network segment?

_____

_____

4.   Your Ethernet network is wired as a physical star. All of the necessary cables are in place. You purchase 50 computers on a sealed bid contract, buying them all from the lowest bidder. When the computers arrive, you discover you have no way of connecting them to the network.

    a.   What kind of device do you need to correct this problem?

_____

_____

    b.   How many will you need?

_____

_____

    c.   How might this problem have been avoided?

_____

_____

5.   Each floor of your office is wired as a 100-Mbps Ethernet network. You have a vertical backbone using UTP cable connecting the floors. You want to keep as much traffic as possible local to each floor and each floor should have a different network address.

    a.   What kind of device should you use to connect each floor to the backbone?

_____

_____

    b.   How is traffic filtered to keep traffic local to the network?

_____

_____

    c.   What kind of network traffic is not propagated by the device?

_____

_____

    d.   How would the requirement change if you had a fiber optic backbone?

_____

_____

6. As your network has grown, network performance has degraded. It dropped significantly when you recently added 50 additional computers. Currently, hubs are used to connect the network computers and all of the hubs are directly connected to each other through uplink ports. You need to correct the problem, but want to avoid reconfiguring the network computers if at all possible. You also want to keep your additional hardware purchases to a minimum.

   a. What kind of device should you use to correct this problem?

   _____

   _____

   b. How would you reconfigure the network?

   _____

   _____

   c. What is the underlying problem and how does this help correct the problem?

   _____

   _____

   d. What changes, if any, must be made to the network computers?

   _____

   _____

7. Your network has four physical segments wired as physical stars. They connect through hubs to a backbone cable. The number of computers on each segment has increased to the point that each needs to be configured as a separate network segment. You want to keep configuration requirements to a minimum.

   a. With what kind of device do you need to replace the hubs?

   _____

   _____

   b. How does this change how traffic is managed by connection devices?

   _____

   _____

   c. What changes, if any, must be made to the network computers?

   _____

   _____

6
NETWORK PROTOCOLS

PROJECTS

Project 6.1	Understanding Key Concepts
Overview	Because term definitions can sometimes vary on the context in which they are used, it is important to be able to recognize terms and how they are used in the context of network protocols. Even the use of the term protocol can somewhat vary, depending on the context.
	The terms presented in this project focus on two types of protocols, access protocols (also called access methods) and network protocols. Access protocols operate at the first two layers of the OSI model. Network protocols, even though most do not map directly to the OSI model, can be considered as operating through the Network layer of the OSI model.
	During this project, you match protocol-related terms to the definitions and descriptions of how they are used.
Outcomes	After completing this project, you will know how to:
	▲ identify key terms and concepts related to access protocols and network protocols
What you'll need	To complete this project, you will need:
	▲ the worksheet below
Completion time	20 minutes
Precautions	None

The worksheet includes a list of network protocol terms on the left and descriptions on the right. Match each term with the description that it most closely matches. You will *not* use all descriptions. Each description can be used only once.

____ Access protocol

A. TCP/IP suite protocol that provides connection-oriented packet delivery services

____ TCP/IP

B. How data is represented on the network for digital transmission as voltage levels or current changes

____ IPX/SPX

C. Bipolar signaling method that always returns to 0V after each +5V or −5V level representing a data bit

____ NWLink

D. IPX/SPX protocol that provides services supporting client/server connections

___ UDP

E. Protocol that operates at the Data Link layer of the OSI model and defines physical media access

___ TCP

F. Dynamically assigned unique computer addresses in an AppleTalk network

___ Encoding method

G. Network protocol used by Novell NetWare 4.0 and earlier

___ XNS

H. Values used with an IP address to identify the network and host portions of the IP address

___ NCP

I. Protocol in the TCP/IP protocol suite that provides connectionless packet delivery services without guarantee of delivery

___ Subnet mask

J. Fixed-size packet

___ Protocol stack

K. Early network protocol used as the basis for the development of many current network protocols

___ Cell

L. Address used to identify a network segment for routing purposes

___ Host address

M. Microsoft equivalent to the IPX/SPX protocol

___ Network address

N. Unique computer address on a network segment in a TCP/IP network

O. The protocols installed on a computer as a protocol suite

P. Network protocol required for Internet access

Project 6.2	Recognizing IEEE Standards
Overview	The network access methods used on PC networks are defined through the IEEE 802 standards. You need to be able to recognize these standards and how each applies to network access requirements. All of the 802 standards are compatible and work together through the Data Link layer of the OSI model.
	During this project you will match some of the most commonly used 802 standards to their descriptions.

Outcomes	After completing this project, you will know how to: ▲ identify IEEE 802.x access standards
What you'll need	To complete this project, you will need: ▲ the worksheet below
Completion time	15 minutes
Precautions	None

The worksheet below lists commonly used 802.x standards. Match each standard to its best description. You will use all of the descriptions.

_____ 802.2

A. Standard that defines the use of fiber optic media in local and metropolitan area networks

_____ 802.3

B. Defines the upper portion of the Data Link layer, known as the Logical Link Control (LLC) sublayer

_____ 802.5

C. Set of standards defining support for wireless technologies and wireless networking with support for communication between two wireless clients and between a client and an access point

_____ 802.7

D. Standard created to define the Token Ring standard developed and trademarked by IBM

_____ 802.8

E. Standard defining support for 100-Mbps transmissions using the Demand Priority Access Method

_____ 802.11

F. Standard specifying the design, installation, and testing necessary for broadband transmissions in a full-duplex medium supporting multiplexing

_____ 802.12

G. Access method that is the standard for Ethernet, based on carrier sense with multiple access and collision detection

Project 6.3	Comparing Protocols
Overview	It is important to understand the various protocols that might be used on a PC network. The protocols include network access protocols, which are implemented through the Data Link level of the OSI model, and network protocols, which are implemented through the Network layer. Even though the term used for each is the same, protocol, they support different features and functionality. During this project, you will identify access and network protocols by their descriptions and features.
Outcomes	After completing this project, you will know how to: ▲ identify network access protocols ▲ identify network communication protocols
What you'll need	To complete this project, you will need: ▲ the worksheet below
Completion time	20 minutes
Precautions	None

■ Part A: Identify network access protocols

Part A includes a table (Table 6-1) with common access protocols and a list of statements that describe one or more of them. Check the boxes for the letters that best describe each access protocol. Each statement applies to at least one access protocol. Some statements may apply to multiple protocols.

A. Determinant access method.

B. Based on 802.11 standards.

C. Uses CSMA/CD.

D. Used in a logical or physical bus topology.

E. Used in a logical or physical ring topology.

F. Based on an IBM trademarked protocol.

G. Most common implementation supports 100 Mbps.

H. By default, can allow unauthorized connections from outside your network.

I. Wired topology access method.

J. Transmission control includes a backoff time.

Table 6-1: Access protocols

Access protocols	A	B	C	D	E	F	G	H	I	J
Token Ring										
Ethernet										
Wireless										

■ Part B: Identify network communication protocols

Part B includes a table (Table 6-2) with common network protocols and a list of statements that describe one or more of them. Check the boxes for the letters that best describe each network protocol. Each statement applies to at least one network protocol. Some statements may apply to multiple protocols.

A. Includes routing support.

B. Required for Internet access.

C. Protocol on which Microsoft's NWLink is based.

D. Also known as DoD protcol suite.

E. Includes a suite of protocols performing various functions.

F. Has two versions known as Phase 1 and Phase 2.

G. Proprietary to Novell.

H. Assembles devices into logical zones.

I. Network and host address are differentiated by a subnet mask.

J. Supports dynamic addressing through DHCP.

Table 6-2: Network protocols

Network protocols	A	B	C	D	E	F	G	H	I	J
TCP/IP										
IPX/SPX										
AppleTalk										

Project 6.4	Installing Network Protocols
Overview	Many operating systems, including Microsoft Windows, give you the option of installing multiple protocol stacks. This expands your options for communicating with different network devices, but at a cost. Each additional protocol stack requires additional memory and processor resources. Currently, most PC networks use TCP/IP as their only protocol. Support for other protocols is implemented either by installing one or more additional protocol stacks or by installing a bridge or gateway that translates between different protocols. When multiple protocols are installed, their relative priority is set through their binding order. During this project you will install additional protocol support for Windows XP and Widows Server 2003.
Outcomes	After completing this project, you will know how to: ▲ install multiple protocols ▲ configure the primary protocol
What you'll need	To complete this project, you will need: ▲ a computer running Windows XP Professional ▲ a computer running Windows Server 2003 ▲ the following worksheet
Completion time	30 minutes
Precautions	If you are doing this project on an existing network, you must review the project steps with your network administrator. Your network administrator may need to make changes or additions to the installation instructions. This project assumes that Control Panel is configured for Classic View.

■ Part A: Explore Windows XP Professional protocol options

Complete this part of the project on the computer running Windows XP Professional.

1. Open the **Control Panel**, select **Network Connections**, and then double-click **Local Area Connection**.

2. Click Properties to open the **Local Area Connection Properties** dialog box similar to the one shown in Figure 6-1.

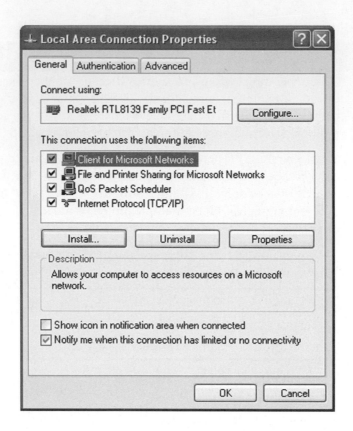

Figure 6-1: Local Area Connection Properties dialog box

3. Review the properties shown on the **General** tab. What protocol stack is currently installed?

    _____

    _____

4. Click Install to display a network component list similar to the one shown in Figure 6-2.

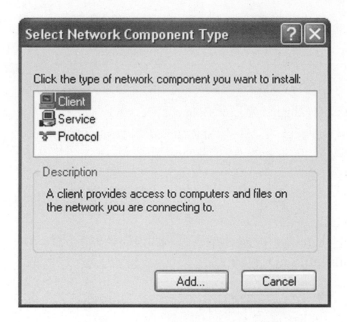

Figure 6-2: Network component list

5. Select **Protocol** and click Add. What options are supported?

_____

_____

_____

6. Select **NWLink** and click OK. What items are added to the local area connection properties?

_____

_____

7. Click OK to close the **Local Area Connection Properties** dialog box.
8. Click Close.

■ Part B: View Windows Server 2003 protocol options

Complete this part of the project on the computer running Windows Server 2003.

1. Open the **Control Panel**, select **Network Connections**, and then double-click **Local Area Connection**.
2. Click Properties to open the **Local Area Connection Properties** dialog box.

3. Review the properties shown on the **General** tab. What protocol stack is currently installed?

    _____

    _____

4. Click Install to display the network component list.
5. Select **Protocol** and click Add. How does this differ from the list seen in Part A?

    _____

    _____

6. Install **NWLink**.
7. Display the available protocols again. Select **AppleTalk** and then click OK.
8. Verify that **AppleTalk** and **NWLink** are installed, as shown in Figure 6-3.

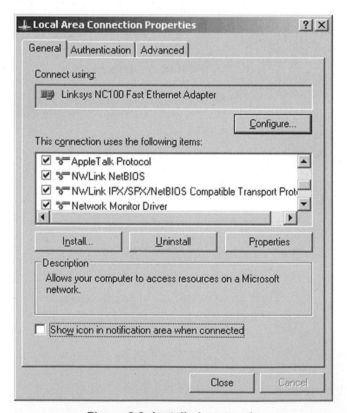

Figure 6-3: Installed protocols

9. Click Close to close the **Local Area Connection Properties** dialog box.
10. Click Close to close the **Network Connections** window.

■ Part C: Configure bindings

You will complete this portion of the project on both computers.

1. On the computer running Windows XP Professional, open the **Control Panel**, right-click **Network Connections**, and then click **Open**.

2. Select **Advanced** and then **Advanced Settings**. This will open an **Advanced Settings** dialog box similar to the one shown in Figure 6-4.

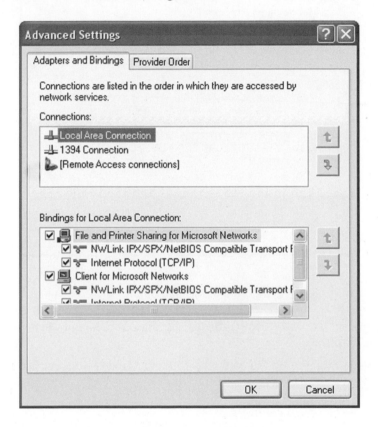

Figure 6-4: Advanced Settings

3. What is the primary protocol for each of the supported services?

_____

4. Under usually networking conditions, what should you have as the primary protocol?

_____

5. Under **File and Printer Sharing for Microsoft Networks**, select **Internet Protocol (TCP/IP)** and click the **Up** arrow. Repeat this for each listed service. When you are finished, the binding should look like Figure 6-5.

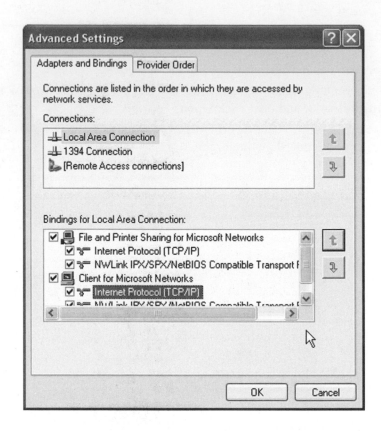

Figure 6-5: Revised bindings

6. Click OK to close the **Advanced Settings** dialog box and then close the **Network Connections** window.

7. Repeat the steps in this part on the computer running Windows Server 2003.

Project 6.5	Comparing Configuration Options
Overview	Just as the features supported vary between different protocol suites, so do the configuration options. You need to understand the options available for each protocol used on your network. You also need to understand how the requirements differ when supporting multiple protocols.

When a protocol is installed, but not needed, you can either uninstall or disable the protocol. If you know that you will not need the protocol in the future, you should uninstall the protocol. If you might have a need, or want to turn off the protocol temporarily, you should disable it through your network connection properties.

During this project you will compare the configuration options supported and will also disable unused protocols. |

Outcomes	After completing this project, you will know how to: ▲ compare protocol configuration options ▲ disable unused protocols
What you'll need	To complete this project, you will need: ▲ a computer running Windows XP Professional ▲ a computer running Windows Server 2003 ▲ the following worksheet
Completion time	30 minutes
Precautions	You must complete Project 6.4 to install the protocols you will configure during this project. If you are doing this project on an existing network, you must review the project steps with your network administrator. Your network administrator may need to make changes or additions to the installation instructions.

■ Part A: Explore protocol configuration options

Complete this part of the project on the computer running Windows Server 2003.

1. Open the **Control Panel**, select **Network Connections**, and then double-click **Local Area Connection**.

2. Click Properties to open the **Local Area Connection Properties** dialog box.

3. Which protocol selection(s) does not have any configurable properties?

   _____

   _____

4. Select **NWLink IPX/SPX/NetBIOS Compatible Transport Protocol** and click Properties. What properties can you configure?

   _____

   _____

5. Select **Manual frame type detection** and then click Add. What parameters, if any, can you configure for each Ethernet frame type?

   _____

   _____

6. Why is this information significant?

   _____

   _____

7. Click Cancel to close the **Manual Frame Detection** dialog box and then click Cancel to close the **NWLink Properties** dialog box, without making any changes.

8. Select **AppleTalk Protocol** and click Properties. What properties can you configure?

_____

_____

9. Click Cancel.

10. Close any open dialog boxes and windows.

■ Part B: Disable protocols

1. On the computer running Windows Server 2003, open the **Local Area Connection Properties** dialog box.

2. Remove the check from **AppleTalk**, **NWLink NetBIOS**, and **NWLink IPX/SPX/NetBIOS Compatible Transport Protocol**, as shown in Figure 6-6.

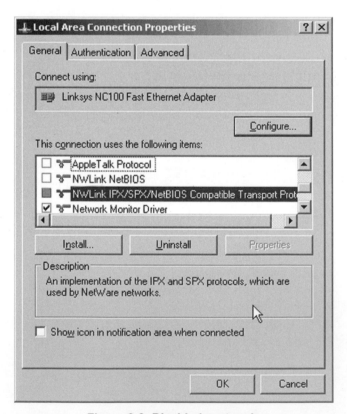

Figure 6-6: Disabled protocols

3. What affect does this have on network communications?

    _____

    _____

    _____

4. What is the advantage of disabling these protocols?

    _____

    _____

    _____

5. Click OK to close the **Local Area Connection Properties** dialog box and save your changes.

6. Use the same procedure to disable **NWLink** support on the computer running Windows XP Professional.

7

TRANSMISSION CONTROL PROTOCOL/INTERNET PROTOCOL (TCP/IP)

PROJECTS

Project 7.1	Understanding Key Concepts
Overview	Due in no small part to the explosive growth of the Internet, TCP/IP has taken over as the de facto network standard over the last several years. Because of this, if you're talking about networks, you're talking TCP/IP. It is important that you can identify TCP/IP terms and the proper context of their use. For many network administrators, this is the only network protocol with which they will ever deal. During this project, you match TCP/IP terms to the definitions and descriptions of how they are used.
Outcomes	After completing this project, you will know how to: ▲ identify key terms and concepts related to TCP/IP
What you'll need	To complete this project, you will need: ▲ the worksheet below
Completion time	20 minutes
Precautions	None

The worksheet includes a list of TCP/IP terms on the left and descriptions on the right. Match each term with the description that it most closely matches. You will *not* use all descriptions. Each description can be used only once.

____	TTL	A. TCP/IP protocol that supports automated IP address and TCP/IP property configuration
____	IP v4	B. Network subnetted to define the boundary for the network and host bits
____	IPv6	C. Canonical name, an alternate name record with the same address as a host A record
____	Classful network	D. DNS record identifying a DNS server
____	Class A	E. TCP/IP utility used to test host-to-host communication
____	Class D	F. Linux/UNIX TCP/IP utility used to retrieve information from, test, and manage name servers
____	NS record	G. Communication test where a computer sends an echo request to itself

____ CNAME record

____ Dig

____ IPconfig

____ Ping

____ Traceroute

____ WINS

____ Loopback

H. Time to live IP header field whose value is used to limit the lifespan of a datagram based on the number of routers (hops) it crosses

I. Linux/UNIX TCP/IP utility that can be used to view and manage IP address and configuration information

J. Linux/UNIX TCP/IP utility used to track a packet from one host to another, including any routers along the way

K. Emerging IP address standard based on 128-bit addresses

L. Windows/MS-DOS TCP/IP utility that can be used to view and manage IP address and configuration information

M. Network address classification defining, by default, up to 127 networks with up to 16,777,214 hosts each

N. The current IP addressing standard based on 32-bit addresses

O. Service used for automated NetBIOS name to IP address resolution on a Windows network

P. Network addresses set aside for multicast applications

Project 7.2	Configuring TCP/IP Properties
Overview	All TCP/IP hosts must have a unique IP address. This can be assigned as a static address, one explicitly specified through the TCP/IP configuration properties, or as a dynamic address, where the host leases an address from a DHCP server. Dynamic addressing is typically used for the majority of the hosts in a TC/IP network, but you need to understand how to configure both dynamic and static addresses. There are also a number of potential security concerns when dealing with DHCP servers, especially in a Windows Active Directory network. Because of this, you will not be setting up and testing DHCP. During this project, you will have an opportunity to review not only address properties, but advanced configuration properties as well.
Outcomes	After completing this project, you will know how to: ▲ configure a host for dynamic address assignment ▲ configure static IP address parameters ▲ configure multihomed addresses
What you'll need	To complete this project, you will need: ▲ a computer running Windows XP Professional ▲ the worksheet below
Completion time	30 minutes
Precautions	This project assumes that you are working on a network that consists on a computer running Windows XP Professional and one computer running Windows Server 2003. Your instructor may provide different instructions if working in a different network configuration. If you are doing this project on an existing network, you must review the project steps with your network administrator. Your network administrator may need to make changes or additions to the project instructions. The project steps assume that you are connected to a wired network. If connected to a wireless network and you have trouble locating the network connection properties, ask your instructor for assistance. The project assumes that the Control Panel on the computer running Windows XP is configured in Classic view.

■ Part A: Record current IP parameters

Complete the following steps in all parts of this project on the computer running Windows XP. You should be logged on as an Administrator. The sample screens in the project do not include the NWLink protocol installed in earlier projects. You do not need NWLink, but there is no reason to remove NWLink at this time.

1. Open the **Start** menu, select **Control Panel**, and double-click **Network Connections**.
2. Double-click **Local Area Connection**.
3. Click Properties to display the **Local Area Connection Properties** dialog box, similar to the example shown in Figure 7-1.

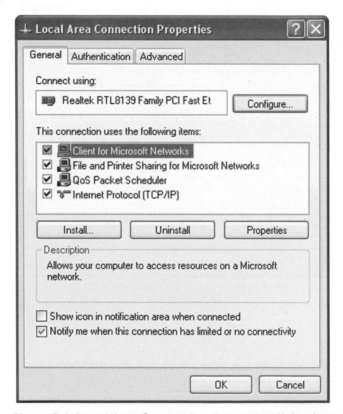

Figure 7-1: Local Area Connection Properties dialog box

4. Select **Internet Protocol (TCP/IP)** and click Properties to display the **Internet Protocol (TCP/IP) Properties** dialog box, similar to that shown in Figure 7-2.

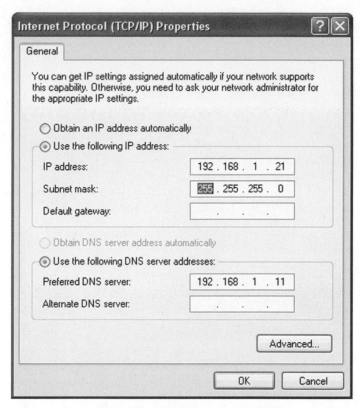

Figure 7-2: General tab in the Internet Protocol (TCP/IP) Properties dialog box

5. Record your current configuration settings below:

IP address: _____

Subnet mask: _____

Default gateway: _____

Preferred DNS server: _____

6. Click Advanced to display the **Advanced TCP/IP Settings** dialog box, similar to that shown in Figure 7-3.

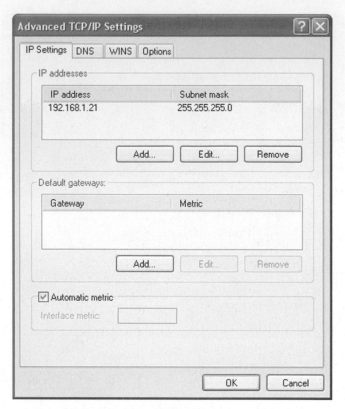

Figure 7-3: Advanced TCP/IP Settings dialog box

7. When would you need to configure a default gateway?

_____

_____

8. Select the **DNS** tab. Review the DNS settings. DNS configuration settings will be covered in detail in a later project.

9. Select the **WINS** tab. Other than broadcast, what NetBIOS name resolution methods are supported by this computer?

_____

10. Is NetBIOS currently enabled?

_____

11. Select the **Options** tab, as shown in Figure 7-4.

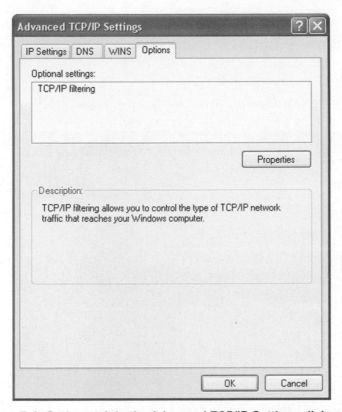

Figure 7-4: Options tab in the Advanced TCP/IP Settings dialog box

12. Click Properties to open the TCP/IP Filtering dialog box. These settings apply to all adapters.

13. What filtering options are currently configured?

_____

_____

14. Click Cancel to close the TCP/IP Filtering dialog box and then click Cancel to close the **Advanced TCP/IP Settings** dialog box. The **Internet Protocol (TCP/IP) Properties** dialog box should still be displayed. Do not close it.

■ Part B: Record current IP parameters

This project assumes you do not have a DCHP server available. You are modifying the settings for practice only.

1. Choose **Obtain an IP address automatically**.

2. How does this change the configuration settings?

_____

3. Choose **Obtain DNS Server address automatically**.

4. How will the computer know what IP address to use?

    _____

5. Select the **Alternate Configuration** tab, as shown in Figure 7-5.

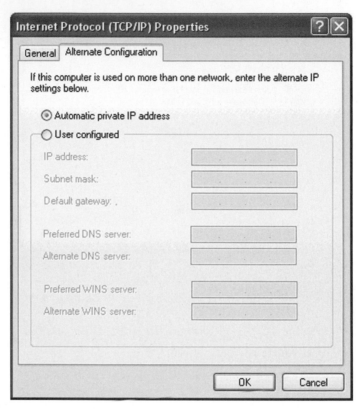

Figure 7-5: Default Alternate Configuration properties

6. When is this configuration used?

    _____

7. What difference would it make if you configure explicit address information?

    _____

8. Select the **General** tab and click Advanced.

9. Review each of the properties settings. How have the IP settings changed?

    _____

10. How have the other tabs in the **Advanced TCP/IP Settings** dialog box changed?

    _____

    _____

11. Click Cancel to close the **Advanced TCP/IP Settings** dialog box. Do not exit the **Internet Protocol (TCP/IP) Properties** dialog box.

■ Part C: Configure a multihomed address

A multihomed address is a host with multiple IP addresses assigned.

1. What happens when you select **Use the following IP address**?

_____

_____

2. Restore the original settings you recorded in Part A of this project. How do you restore this information?

_____

3. Click Advanced.

4. Click Add to open the **TCP/IP Address** dialog box, as shown in Figure 7-6.

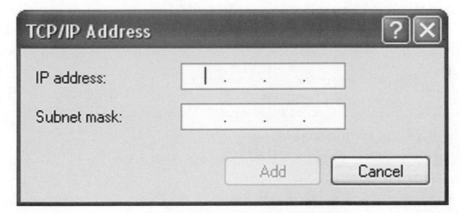

Figure 7-6: TCP/IP Address dialog box

5. Enter **192.168.10.144**, or other address provided by your instructor, in the **IP address** box, and press the Tab key. What happens?

_____

6. Click Add. Your IP address properties should look like the example shown in Figure 7-7.

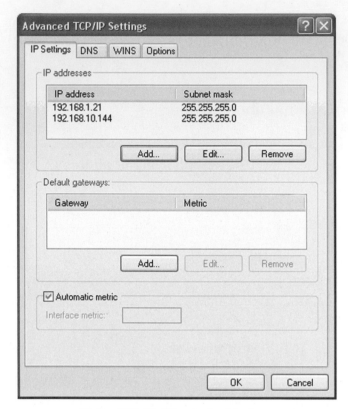

Figure 7-7: Multihomed addresses

7. Click OK. How have the general properties changed?

   _____

8. Click OK to save the TCP/IP property changes.

9. Click Close to close the **Local Area Connection Properties** dialog box. Click Close to close the **Network Connections** window.

10. Open the **Start** menu, select **Run**, enter **cmd** in the **Open** field, and then click Open to open a command prompt.

11. Enter **ipconfig** in the command prompt.

12. What IP address or addresses are returned?

    _____

13. Exit the command prompt.

Project 7.3	Comparing Name Resolution Options
Overview	Name resolution, associating computer names with IP addresses, is a critical function in a TCP/IP network. Name resolution lets you locate hosts by name.
	There are two types of name systems used, DNS names and NetBIOS names. DNS names are the types of names used across the Internet. A DNS name is made up of the host's unique name with the domain name as a suffix, like student00.busicorp.com.
	The other type of name system used is NetBIOS names, which are simple text names used with NetBIOS applications and the NetBEUI network protocol, like STUDENT00.
	Name resolution is managed through name servers and text files. DNS names are resolved using DNS servers and the HOSTS file. NetBIOS names, in a Windows network, are resolved using WINS servers and the LMHOSTS file. LMHOSTS can also be used with other network types. For local name resolution, hosts on the same subnetwork, NetBIOS names can also be resolved through broadcasts.
	In this project, you will answer questions related to name resolution scenarios.
Outcomes	After completing this project, you will know how to:
	▲ identify DNS resolution options and parameters
	▲ identify WINS resolution options and parameters
What you'll need	To complete this project, you will need:
	▲ the worksheet below
Completion time	30 minutes
Precautions	None

■ Part A: DNS name resolution

Part A is based on the network shown in Figure 7-8. The DNS server named dns1.busicorp.com is the authoritive name server for the domain. The server dns2.busicorp.com is updated periodically with information from dns1.busicrop.com. Hosts can use either name server to resolve host names. You want to keep traffic related to name resolution to a minimum. The computer linux.busicorp.com is configured as a router.

Note: In a real-world configuration, you would probably give your DNS servers less obvious names to help prevent them from being compromised.

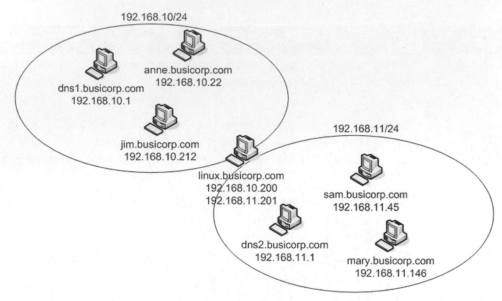

Figure 7-8: DNS resolution sample

1. How would you configure the primary and alternate DNS servers for sam.busicorp.com and jim.busicorp.com and why?

   a.sam.busicorp.com

   Primary DNS server: _____

   Alternate DNS server: _____

   b. jim.busicorp.com

   Primary DNS server: _____

   Alternate DNS server: _____

   Reason:

   _____

   _____

4. To which DNS server would you make updates?

   _____

5. Why?

   _____

6. Why shouldn't you make updates to the other DNS server?

   _____

   _____

   _____

7. What special configuration requirements are there for linux.busicorp.com to support name resolution?

_____

8. If the following is run from sam.busicorp.com, it succeeds:

    ```
    ping 192.168.11.146
    ```
    If the following is run, it succeeds:
    ```
    ping anne.busicorp.com:
    ```
    If the following is run, it fails:
    ```
    ping mary.busicorp.com
    ```
    If you run the same commands from jim.busicorp.com, you get the same symptoms. What is most likely wrong, and how did you determine this?

_____

_____

_____

_____

_____

9. This is a separate scenario. Do not consider the errors reported in question 4.

    The only computer experiencing problems is anne.busicorp.com. When you run the following, it succeeds:

    ```
    ping jim.busicorp.com
    ```
    If you run the following, it fails:
    ```
    ping mary.busicorp.com
    ```
    If you run the following, it fails:
    ```
    ping sam.busicorp.com
    ```
    If you run the same commands from any other computer, they all succeed. What is most likely wrong, and how did you determine this?

_____

_____

_____

_____

_____

■ Part B: Mixed name resolution

Part B is based on the network shown in Figure 7-9. The network is a Windows Active Directory domain with the domain controllers identified in the figure. The domain controllers are configured as DNS servers. The computer named sppt.busicorp.com will be configured as a WINS proxy server. This means that it forwards NetBIOS name resolution requests to the WINS server and returns the result to the local subnetwork. The computer linux.busicorp.com is configured as a router.

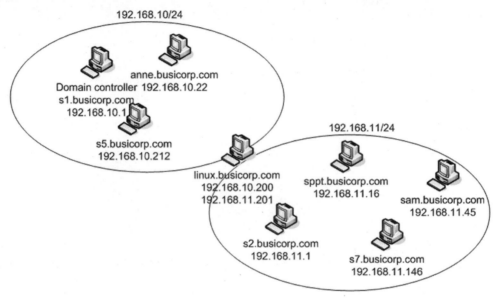

Figure 7-9: Mixed name resolution

1. What would justify configuring NetBIOS name resolution?

   _____

   _____

   _____

2. If configuring a WINS server, which server should you use (s5.busicorp.com or s7.busicorp.com)?

   _____

3. Why?

   _____

   _____

4. How can you avoid having computers running Windows XP to use the WINS proxy server?

    _____

    _____

5. How would you do this?

    _____

    _____

6. Assuming you do not want to configure a WINS server, how could you support NetBIOS name resolution for computers on the local network?

    _____

    _____

7. How could you support NetBIOS name resolution for computers on the remote network?

    _____

    _____

Project 7.4	Comparing Name Resolution Methods
Overview	The specific requirements for configuring name resolution depend on whether you need to support DNS names or both NetBIOS names and DNS names. They also vary depending on how you are managing name resolution.
	A DNS server is the preferred method on most networks. However, there are also situations in which you need to use HOSTS file name resolution. Because of this, you need to understand how to set up and how to use both resolution methods.
	This project takes a closer look at DNS configuration options and tests using a HOSTS files for name resolution.
Outcomes	After completing this project, you will know how to:
	▲ view DNS server properties
	▲ configure DNS client properties
	▲ modify and use a HOSTS file
What you'll need	To complete this project, you will need:
	▲ a computer running Windows XP Professional
	▲ a computer running Windows Server 2003
	▲ the following worksheet

Completion time	30 minutes
Precautions	This project assumes that you are working on a network that consists of a computer running Windows Server2003 configured as a domain controller and a computer running Windows XP Professional configured as a domain member. Your instructor may provide different instructions if working in a different network configuration.
	If you are doing this project on an existing network, you must review the project steps with your network administrator. Your network administrator may need to make changes or additions to the project instructions.
	This project assumes that the Control Panel is configured for Classic View.

■ Part A: DNS server properties

Complete this part of the project on the computer running Windows Server 2003. You must be logged on as an Administrator.

1. Why was it necessary to configure this computer as a DNS server when promoting the server to domain controller?

    _____

    _____

2. Open the **Start** menu, point to **Administrative Tools**, and then select **DNS**.
3. Expand your **server** and **Forward Lookup Zones**, and then select **BUSICORP.COM**, as shown in Figure 7-10.

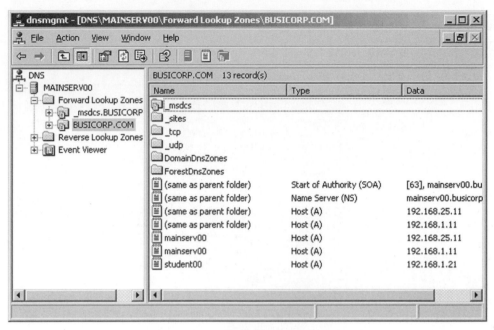

Figure 7-10: BUSICORP.COM zone

4. What computers are listed?

    _____

    _____

5. Look closely at Figure 7-10. How do the domain controller's TCP/IP configuration properties differ from your computer, assuming your domain controller is configured as specified in earlier projects?

    _____

6. How can you tell this?

    _____

7. From the information in the DNS table, how can you tell that the domain controller is a DNS server?

    _____

8. Is it required in any network configuration that each domain controller also be configured as a DNS server?

    _____

9. In the tree view on the left, select **Event Viewer**. This displays entries related to DNS only. You should see one or more errors listed, as in Figure 7-11.

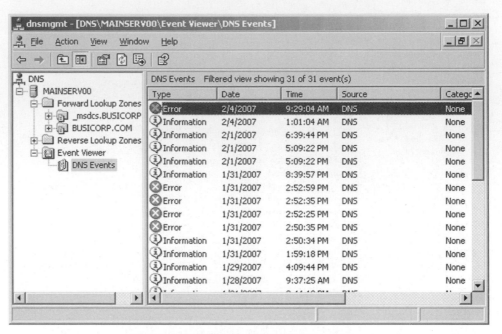

Figure 7-11: DNS server event log entries

10. Double-click the most recent error to view error details. They should be similar to the example shown in Figure 7-11. Why did this error occur?

_____

_____

_____

11. Close all open windows.

■ **Part B: View name resolution configuration**

You will complete this portion of the project on the computer running Windows XP Professional.

1. Open the **Internet Protocol (TCP/IP) Properties** dialog box for your computer. Refer to the steps in Project 7.2 if necessary.

2. What computer is configured as the DNS server?

_____

3. Click Advanced.

4. Select the **DNS** tab.

5. Which configuration option enables this computer to register itself with the DNS server?

_____

6. What term refs to this DNS feature?

_____

7. Click Cancel. Do not close the **Internet Protocol (TCP/IP) Properties** dialog box.

■ Part C: Test name resolution options

You will complete this portion of the project on the computer running Windows XP Professional.

1. Open a command prompt and execute the following: **ping *domain_controller*.** (Replace domain_controller with your domain controller's fully qualified name.)

2. How did your computer get the remote computer's address?

_____

3. In the **Internet Protocol (TCP/IP) Properties** dialog box, delete the DNS server address so that no DNS server is defined, as shown in Figure 7-12.

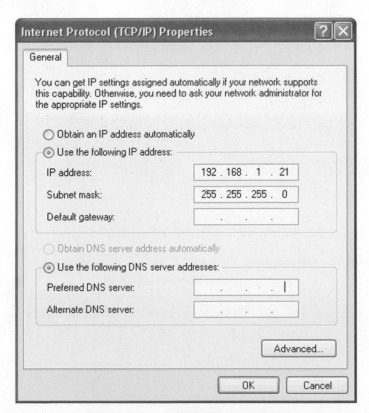

Figure 7-12: No DNS Server defined

4. Click OK and then close the **Local Area Connection Properties** dialog box to apply the changes.

5. In the command prompt, execute the following to remove any cached name resolution information: **ipconfig /flushdns**.

6. Repeat step 1 to ping your domain controller. What happens?

_____

7. Why?

_____

8. Open **My Computer** and navigate to the following location: **c:\WINDOWS\system32\drivers\etc**.

   Note: This assumes that Windows XP was installed to the default location. If not, use the path to the installation destination.

9. Double-click **hosts**. When prompted for the program you want to use, select **Notepad** and click OK.

10. The file should look like the sample shown in Figure 7-13.

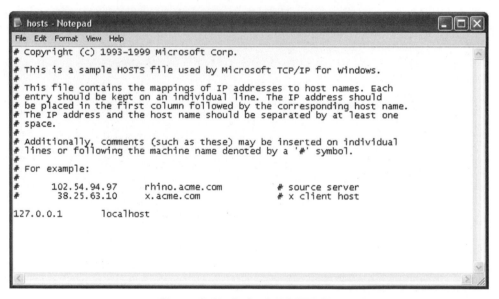

Figure 7-13: Default HOSTS file

11. Edit the file to add your domain controller. A sample is shown in Figure 7-14.

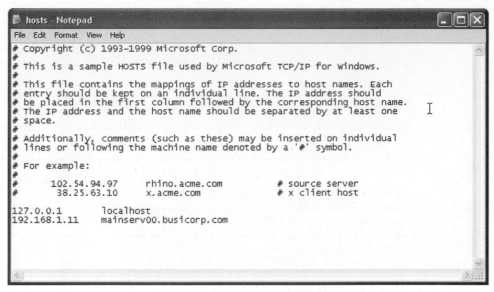

Figure 7-14: Edited HOSTS file

12. Select **File**, click **Save** to save your changes, and then exit **Notepad**.

13. In the command prompt, ping your domain controller. What happens?

_____

14. Why?

_____

15. Open your computer's **Internet Protocol (TCP/IP) Properties** dialog box and restore the DNS server properties to their original settings.

16. Close all open windows.

Project 7.5	Designing Subnetworks
Overview	Subnetworking is the process of dividing a network address into smaller networks. The more the subnetworks you create, the fewer hosts per subnetwork are supported. The subnet mask determines which bits are used for the network address and which are used for the host address.

To understand the available host addresses, you have to consider the binary host address values. There are two values that cannot be used as host addresses. The host bits cannot be set to all zeros, because this is the network address. The host bits also cannot be set to all ones, because this is the broadcast address. Packets sent to the broadcast address are processed by all hosts on the subnetwork. Routers do not pass broadcast packets. |

	In the project, you will be presented with subnet scenarios and graphic representations of network configurations. You will be asked questions about each scenario.
Outcomes	After completing this project, you will know how to: ▲ design subnetworks to meet network configuration requirements ▲ determine the available addresses for a network
What you'll need	To complete this project, you will need: ▲ the following worksheet
Completion time	45 minutes
Precautions	None. You can use the Windows calculator in Scientific mode to convert between binary and decimal values.

■ Part A: Scenario #1

All of the questions in this scenario refer to Figure 7-15. Each subnet must support at least 50 host computers. There are no plans in the near future to expand the network. You have the class C address 201.14.2 available for subnetting.

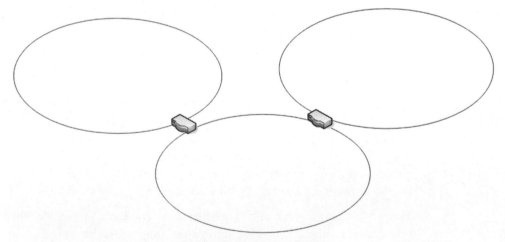

Figure 7-15: Scenario #1

1. What subnet mask should you use?

_____

2. Why?

_____

3. At minimum, how many IP addresses must be configured for each router?

_____

4. Why?

_____

5. For each possible network, what are the network address and broadcast address?

_____

_____

_____

_____

■ Part B: Scenario #2

All of the questions in this scenario refer to Figure 7-16. The number inside each subnet is the network address. These addresses were derived by subnetting the class C address 211.1.44. Each network must support at least 16 hosts.

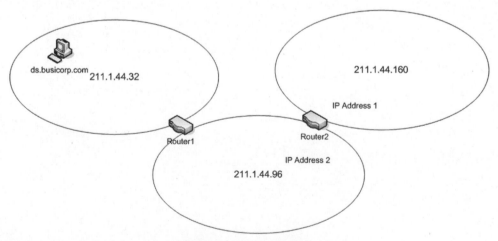

Figure 7-16: Scenario 2

1. What subnet mask would you use with this configuration?

_____

2. How many additional network addresses are available that are not used?

_____

3. How many hosts can each subnet support?

_____

4. You want to address Router2 with the first valid host address in each connected network. What addresses should you use?

_____

_____

5. You want to configure ds.busicorp.com with the numerically highest available host address. What should you use?

_____

6. The network does not use WINS servers. NetBIOS support is needed on network number 211.1.44.96 only. If a host is attempting to resolve a NetBIOS address, to what IP address would it address the request?

_____

7. Why?

_____

_____

8. For each of the following addresses, identify it as being on network number 211.1.44.32, 211.1.44.96, 211.1.44.160, or invalid (not supported on any subnetwork).

211.1.44.190   _____

211.1.44.187   _____

211.1.44.40   _____

211.1.44.65   _____

211.1.44.94   _____

211.1.44.170   _____

211.1.44.131   _____

8

WIRELESS, REMOTE, AND WIDE AREA NETWORKING

PROJECTS

Project 8.1	Understanding Key Concepts
Overview	Remote access and wide area networks (WANs) have been part of PC networking since its first days, based initially on technologies used to support remote mainframe technology. Wireless networking is a more recent, but not less important, addition to the networking mix. Part of preparing to support different networking options is understanding related terms. Each different networking configuration has its own related terms, many of which depend on the context in which they are used. During this project, you match various networking terms to the definitions and descriptions of how they are used.
Outcomes	After completing this project, you will know how to: ▲ identify key terms and concepts related to TCP/IP
What you'll need	To complete this project, you will need: ▲ the worksheet below
Completion time	20 minutes
Precautions	None

The worksheet includes a list of networking terms on the left and descriptions on the right. Match each term with the description that it most closely matches. You will *not* use all descriptions. Each description can be used only once.

___ PPP

A. Access method used on Wi-Fi networks. It is similar to the CSMA/CD used on Ethernet networks, except that it makes more of an effort to avoid collisions between transmitting devices

___ L2TP

B. Telephone network and infrastructure that includes the standard dial-up phone network

___ BRI

C. Circuit-switched network communication method that combines voice, video, and data communication

___ CSMA/CA

D. Protocol used for remote client connections over a variety of connection methods and supporting multiple network protocols

___ ISDN

E. Microsoft service that supports routing, remote access, and virtual private network (VPN) access

___   X.25

F.   Packet-switched   network   standard communication method that provides improved performance compared to X.25, scalable up to 39 Gbps

___   T-carrier circuit

G. ANSI standard high-speed United States fiber-based communication network

___   SONET

H. Media access method in which a device must physically listen before transmitting

___   RRAS

I. Industry-standard VPN connection protocol

___   PSTN

J. ISDN connection device that acts like a hub for ISDN connections

___   Packet-switched network

K. Oldest packet-switched service in current use

___   NT1/NT2

L. Most common type of dedicated circuit service

___   DCF

M. Packet-switched network connection device

___   PAD

N. Cloud architecture carrier network using fixed-rate connection plus per packet charges to determine charges

O. Transmission method that transmits data faster than X.25, but slower than ATM, but does not include any error control

P. ISDN configuration that has two B channels and one D channel

Project 8.2	Understanding Wireless Technologies
Overview	Wireless networking has become the preferred network topology in several networking scenarios. Development of wireless networking technologies is moving more quickly than other technologies that relate to PC networking. Because of this, if you aren't dealing with wireless networking now, you probably will be soon. One of the problems with a technology that is changing and expanding this quickly is simply keeping up with the current state of the technology. Another is understanding how to properly deploy wireless networking and how it impacts existing wired networks. During this project, you will review various wireless technologies and some important considerations related to wireless access point (WAP) configuration.
Outcomes	After completing this project, you will know how to: ▲ identify wireless standards and their use ▲ configure wireless support
What you'll need	To complete this project, you will need: ▲ the worksheet below
Completion time	30 minutes
Precautions	None

■ Part A: Wireless transmission standards

The worksheet below lists commonly used 802.x wireless standards. Match each standard to its best description. You will use all of the descriptions.

____ 802.11a

      A. Fixed WiMAX, sometimes used for MAN connections or to connect public Wi-Fi WAPs to a central point

____ 802.11b

      B. Emerging standard that uses both 2.4- and 5-GHz ranges and is expected to support speeds up to 240 Mbps

___   802.11g   C. Standard that operates in the 5-GHz range, but not commonly used in PC networking

___   802.11n   D. Mobile WiMAX, designed as an alternative networking standard for cell phones and computer hardware

___   802.16d   E. Current and most commonly used Wi-Fi networking standard

___   802.16e   F. Original Wi-Fi networking standard

■ Part B: Wireless network configuration

You are configuring a network that will include wireless device support. The network design calls for 150 devices, 100 of which will be wireless devices. You need to allow for a potential 10% growth. The majority of the devices receive their TCP/IP configuration information automatically. The wired and wireless devices should all be part of the same network segment.

You decide to bring in three high-speed Internet lines to provide connectivity for both wired and wireless devices. You plan to install three WAPs that also act as routers and include NAT functionality to support both wireless clients and wired Internet access. DHCP service support is built into the WAPs and enabled by default. DHCP provides all general IP configuration parameters for clients leasing addresses. The WAPs support configurable private Class C addresses for intranet addresses. You can change the address range, but not the Class C address network address.

Answer the following questions related to wireless network configuration and interaction between wired and wireless networking.

1. What will act as the TCP/IP default gateway for wireless clients in this configuration?

   _____

2. What will act as the TCP/IP default gateway for wired clients in this configuration?

   _____

3. WAPs receive Internet IP addressing parameters from the Internet Service Provider (ISP) through DHCP. What are the concerns when configuring local IP address information for the WAPs?

   _____

4. The network will have 10 wired servers that require static IP addresses. What guidelines should you consider when assigning IP address and subnet information?

_____

_____

5. For servers that need Internet access, what should you use as the default gateway?

_____

6. How can you find values to use for Internet DNS servers?

_____

_____

7. Each WAP has four RJ-45 connectors for wired clients. How can you configure the network to support the necessary number of wired clients?

_____

_____

8. How can you prevent DHCP on the three WAPs from trying to assign duplicate addresses?

_____

■ Part C: Wireless access point configuration

This part uses the same network scenario as Part B. You are answering specific questions about DCHP and network configuration, but in the context of WAP configuration. Many of the issues discussed here would also apply to the DCHP service running on a wired server. Using the configuration screen shown in Figure 8-1, answer the following questions about WAP configuration:

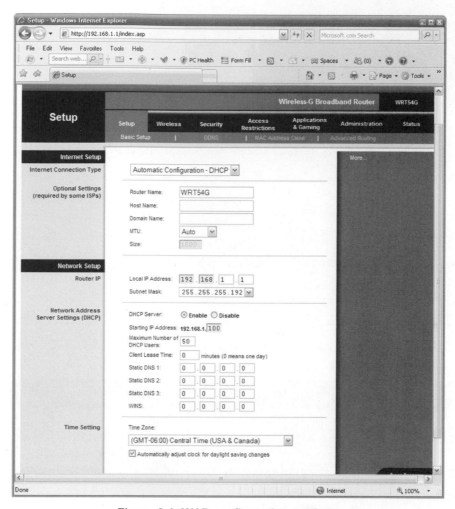

Figure 8-1: WAP configuration settings

1. The Router IP settings let you set the last two dotted decimal values and select the subnet mask from the standard subnet masks supported for Class C networks. Will it be necessary to change these configuration settings, and if so, how?

_____

_____

_____

2. Configuring the Router IP and DHCP settings, what is the potential problem if you change both of the last two dotted decimal values in the Router IP address?

_____

_____

_____

_____

3. What wireless standard or standards will this WAP support?

_____

_____

4. How would you need to change the starting IP address and maximum DHCP users, if at all?

_____

_____

_____

Project 8.3	Setting up Remote Access
Overview	Windows Server 2003 Routing and Remote Access (RRAS) allows you to configure a server to support dial-up and VPN remote access connections. RRAS supports both PPTP and L2TP VPN connections. The same server can support multiple clients; however, a separate dial-up modem is needed for each dial-up client.
	Under normal circumstances, you would normally not install RRAS on a domain controller. This would be a potential security hole. For the purposes of this lab and because of your limited number of computers, we will make an exception.
	In this project, you will enable RRAS on a computer running Windows Server 2003 and view its configuration.
Outcomes	After completing this project, you will know how to:
	▲ enable RRAS
	▲ configure dial-up and VPN client support
What you'll need	To complete this project, you will need:
	▲ a computer running Windows Server 2003
Completion time	20 minutes
Precautions	The instructions in this project assume you are working on a two-node network with one computer running Windows XP Professional and one computer running Windows Server 2003. If these computers are part of a

larger classroom network, your instructor will provide you with alternate instructions for configuring network and domain parameters. Depending on the classroom network configuration, your instructor may decide to have you work in groups to configure remote access.

If working on an existing network, you must review the project steps with your network administrator. Your network administrator may need to make changes or additions to the instructions.

■ Part A: Enable routing and remote access

In this part of the project, you will enable RRAS for both dial-up and VPN connections. You will assign IP addresses from a static pool. You will need to be logged on to the computer running Windows Server 2003 as Administrator at the beginning of this part of the project.

Steps 1 through 4 are specific to a wired connection. If you have a wireless connection and need help displaying connection properties, ask you instructor for assistance.

1. Open the **Start** menu, select **Control Panel**, select **Network Connections**, and then select **Local Area Connection**.

2. Click Properties to display the **Local Area Connection Properties** dialog box (Figure 8-2).

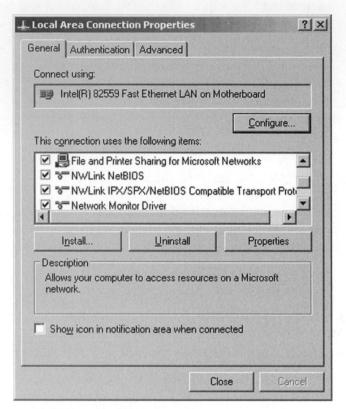

Figure 8-2: Connection properties

3. If your computer has **NWLink** or **AppleTalk** installed, as shown in Figure 8-2, for each of the protocols:

   a. Click to select the protocol.

   b. Click Uninstall.

   c. Click Yes if prompted to verify your action.

   Note: Do not remove **Network Monitor Driver**.

4. Click Close to close the **Local Area Connection Properties** dialog box and then click Close to close the **Network Connections** window.

5. Open the **Start** menu, point to **All Programs** and then to **Administrative Tools**, and select **Routing and Remote Access** to open the **Routing and Remote Access** console, as shown in Figure 8-3.

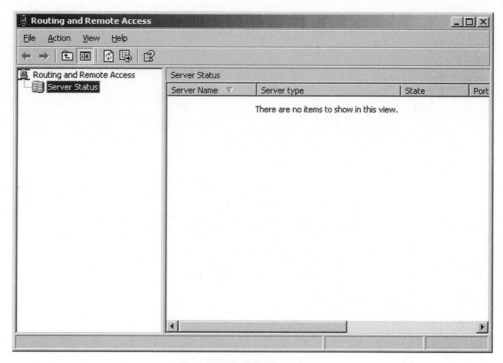

Figure 8-3: RRAS console

Note: You can also configure a computer as a remote access server by using the **Manage Your Server** utility to add the **Remote Access/VPN Server** role. The configuration wizard steps are the same in either case.

6. If your server is not listed, right-click **Server Status** and select **Add Server**.

7. Leave the default, **This computer**, selected and click OK.

8. Right-click your server and select **Configure and Enable Routing and Remote Access**.

9. Click Next.

10. Keep the default selection, **Remote Access (dial-up or VPN)** (see Figure 8-4), and click Next.

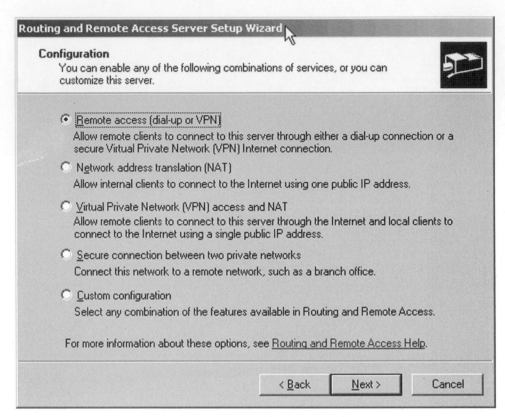

Figure 8-4: Configuring remote access

11. Select **VPN** and **Dial-up**, as shown in Figure 8-5, and click Next.

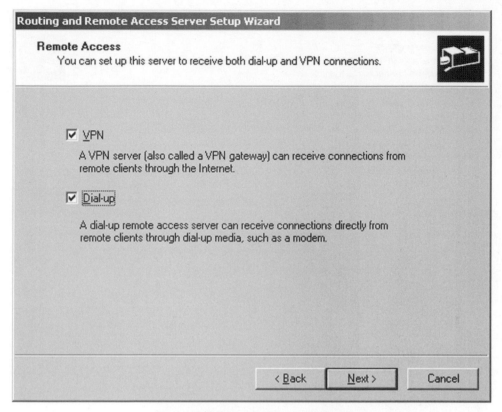

Figure 8-5: Select VPN and Dial-up

12. Select the **Local Area Connection** interface.

13. Remove the check from **Enable security on the selected interface by setting up static packet filters**, as shown in Figure 8-6.

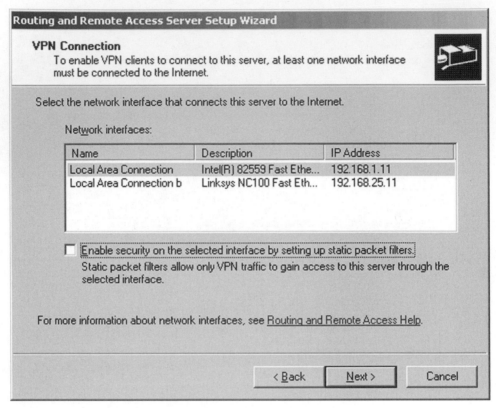

Figure 8-6: Disable packet filter security

14. Click Next.

15. Select **From a specified range of addresses** to configure the server to assign IP addresses from a pool. Click Next..

16. Why do you need to assign address from a specific range of addresses?

_____

_____

17. Click New to display the **New Address Range** dialog box.

18. Click New, enter **192.168.1.200** as the start address and **192.168.1.209** as the end address, as shown in Figure 8-7, and click OK.

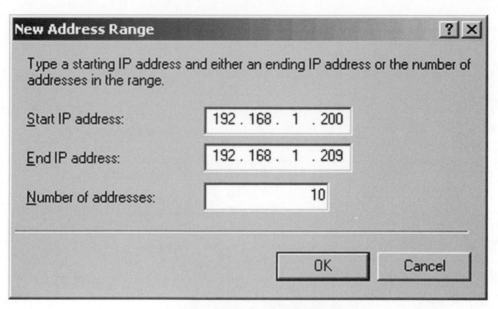

Figure 8-7: New Address Range dialog box

19. Click Next.

20. Keep the default selection **No, use Routing and Remote Access to authenticate connection requests** and click Next.

21. What benefit would you gain by using RADIUS?

   _____

22. Review the configuration and click Finish.

23. When prompted with the warning about the DHCP Relay Agent, click OK.

24. Why doesn't the DHCP Relay Agent warning apply?

   _____

25. If necessary, after the **Routing and Remote Access Server** service starts, click Finish.

26. How does the **Routing and Remote Access** console visually indicate that the service is running?

   _____

27. Do not close the **Routing and Remote Access** console.

■ **Part B: View the remote access server configuration**

In this part of the project, you will view the configuration for the remote access server.

1. Expand **Mainserv00**, as shown in Figure 8-8.

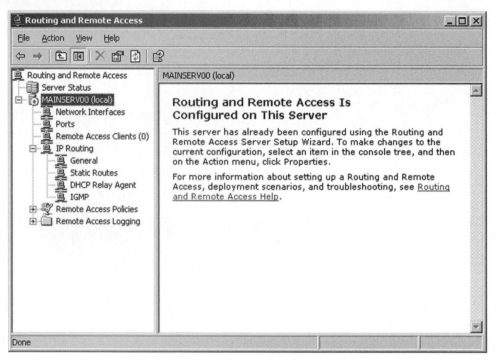

Figure 8-8: Server information

2. Right-click **Mainserv00** and choose **Properties** to display the **Properties** dialog box for the server, as shown in Figure 8-9.

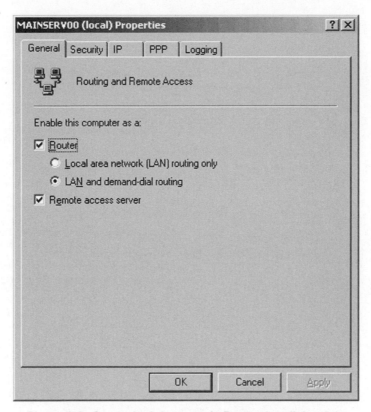

Figure 8-9: General tab in server's Properties dialog box

3. What configuration is supported?

    _____

    _____

4. Display the **Security** tab, as shown in Figure 8-10.

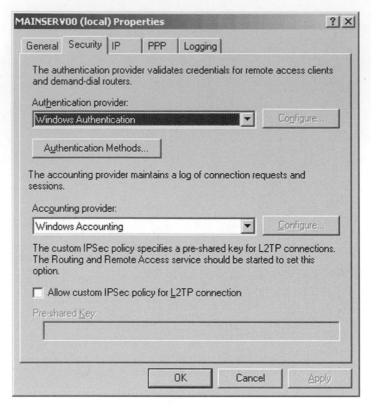

Figure 8-10: Security tab

5. Click Authentication Methods.
6. What authentication methods are enabled by default?

_____

7. Click Cancel.
8. Display the **IP** tab, as shown in Figure 8-11.

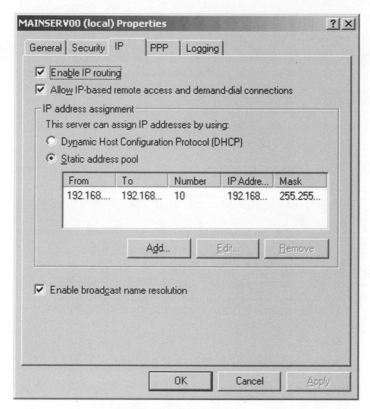

Figure 8-11: IP tab

9. Click Cancel to close the **Properties** dialog box.

10. Right-click **Ports** and choose **Properties**.

11. What network ports are listening?

_____

12. Click Cancel to close the **Ports Properties** dialog box.

13. Close the **Routing and Remote Access** console.

Project 8.4	Configuring a Dial-up Client
Overview	Windows XP Professional can be configured to support both incoming and outgoing dial-up connections. You will want to be cautious when configuring an incoming dial-up connection because it is an entry point to your computer from anywhere with a phone line. This is particularly true if your computer is connected to a network. Part of the configuration process is configuring a network user account to enable dial-up access for that user. Only those users who have a need for remote access should be enabled. Each user for whom you allow remote access is a potential security hole if someone else gets the account information. In this project you will configure a dial-up connection. You will not be able to test it unless you have a modem and another computer with a modem.
Outcomes	After completing this project, you will know how to: ▲ configure a dial-up connection on Windows XP Professional ▲ create and configure a user for dial-up access
What you'll need	To complete this project, you will need: ▲ a domain controller running Windows Server 2003 ▲ a Windows XP Professional domain member
Completion time	30 minutes
Precautions	The instructions in this project assume you are working on a two-node network with one computer running Windows XP Professional and one computer running Windows Server 2003. If these computers are part of a larger classroom network, your instructor will provide you with alternate instructions for configuring network and domain parameters. If working on an existing network, you must review the project steps with your network administrator. Your network administrator may need to make changes or additions to the instructions.

■ Part A: Set dial-in properties on a user account

In this part of the project, you will create and configure a user account so that the user can dial in to the remote access server. You will perform this part of the project on the computer running Windows Server 2003.

1. Open the **Start** menu, point to **All Programs** and then to **Administrative Tools**, and select **Active Directory Users and Computers**.
2. If necessary, expand **BUSICORP.COM**.

3. Right-click **Users**, and select **New** and then **User** to display the **New Object-User** dialog box.

4. Complete the **New Object-User** dialog box, as shown in Figure 8-12, with user name **Ron User** and logon name **RUser**, and click Next.

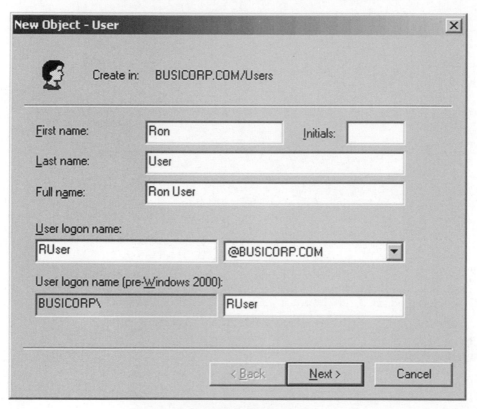

Figure 8-12: New user

5. Enter **P*ssword** in the **Password** and **Confirm password** fields, remove the check from **User must change password at next login**, and click Next.

6. Click Finish.

7. Select the **User OU**, locate and right-click **Ron User**, and select **Properties**.

8. Display the **Dial-in** tab, as shown in Figure 8-13.

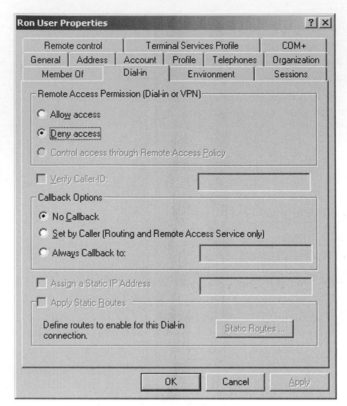

Figure 8-13: Dial-in tab

9. What is the default setting?

_____

10. Select **Allow access**.
11. Click OK to close the **Properties** dialog box.
12. Close **Active Directory Users and Computers**.

■ Part B: Configure a dial-up connection

In this part of the project, you will view configure a dial-up connection on the computer running Windows XP Professional. You must perform this part of the project logged on as Administrator on the computer running Windows XP Professional. These steps assume that your **Control Panel** is configured for **Classic View**.

1. Open the **Start** menu and select **Control Panel**.
2. Double-click **Network Connections**.
3. In the **Network Tasks** pane, click **Create a new connection**, as shown in Figure 8-14.

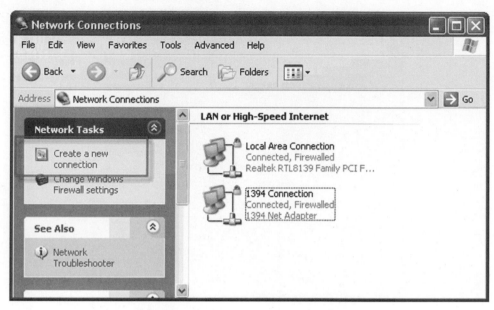

Figure 8-14: Creating a new connection

4. If you have not set up a previous dial-up connection or configured phone and modem options, a dialog box will display prompting you for location information. Enter the information relevant to your phone line and click OK. If you are not prompted for this information, continue with step 7.

5. Click OK to close **Phone and Modem Options**.

6. On the **Welcome** screen of **New Connection Wizard**, click Next.

7. Select **Connect to the network at my workplace**. Click Next.

8. Leave **Dial-up connection** selected and click Next.

9. Enter **Busicorp Office** as the company name and click Next.

10. Enter **18885551212** as the phone number and click Next.

11. Keep **Anyone's use** selected and click Next.

12. Give an example of when you might select **My use only** instead.

_____

_____

13. Review your configuration and click Finish.

14. If you have a modem installed, a dialog box like the one shown in Figure 8-15 will dislay. You must enter the user name and password to use for authentication. Click Cancel to close the dialog box.

Figure 8-15: Connection dialog box

15. Why doesn't computer fill in the user name automatically with the current user?

_____

_____

16. Verify that your new connection is listed, as shown in Figure 8-16.

Figure 8-16: New dial-up connection

Note: If you do not have a modem installed, the dial-up connection will be created, but will be marked as unavailable.

17. Close **Network Connections**.

Project 8.5	Configuring a VPN Client
Overview	A remote user with a broadband Internet connection can be configured to connect to a LAN securely by tunneling through the Internet. This is known as a virtual private network (VPN). Windows XP Professional supports both PPTP and L2TP/IPsec VPN connections.
	In this project you will configure a VPN connection on the Windows XP Professional computer.
Outcomes	After completing this project, you will know how to:
	▲ configure a VPN connection
	▲ connect using a VPN connection
What you'll need	To complete this project, you will need:
	▲ domain controller running Windows Server 2003
	▲ domain member running Windows XP Professional
	▲ to have completed Project 8.3 and Project 8.4
Completion time	15 minutes
Precautions	The instructions in this project assume you are working on a two-node network with one computer running Windows XP Professional and one computer running Windows Server 2003. If these computers are part of a larger classroom network, your instructor will provide you with alternate

> instructions for configuring network and domain parameters.
>
> If working on an existing network, you must review the project steps with your network administrator. Your network administrator may need to make changes or additions to the instructions.

■ Part A: Create a VPN connection

In this part of the project, you will create a VPN connection on the computer running Windows XP Professional. You must be logged on as Administrator. These steps assume the **Control Panel** is configured in **Classic View**.

1. Open the **Start** menu and select the **Control Panel**.
2. Double-click **Network Connections**.
3. In the **Network Tasks** pane, click **Create a new connection**.
4. On the **Welcome** screen, click Next.
5. Select **Connect to the network at my workplace** and click Next.
6. Select **Virtual Private Network connection** and click Next.
7. Enter **Busicorp via I-net** as the **Company Name** and click Next.
8. Select the **Do not dial the initial** connection and click Next.
9. When can you choose this connection option?

   _____

   _____

10. Enter **mainserv00.busicorp.com** (or your domain controller name, if different) as the server name and click Next.
11. Keep **My use only** selected and click Next.
12. Click Finish to create the connection.
13. In the **Connect Busicorp via I-net** dialog box, enter **Adminstrator** as the **User name** and **P*ssword** as the password, as shown in Figure 8-17.

Figure 8-17: Connecting as Administrator

14. What happens?

_____

_____

15. Click Cancel.
16. Double-click **Busicorp via I-net**.
17. Enter **RUser** as the user name and **P*ssword** as the password, and click Connect.
18. Right-click the connection and choose **Status**.
19. Display the **Details** tab, as shown in Figure 8-18.

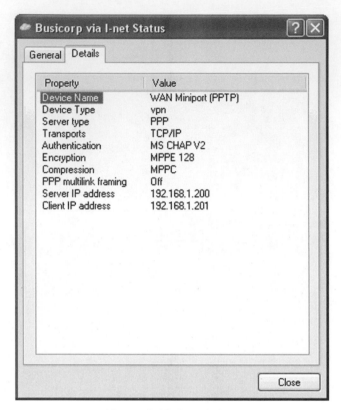

Figure 8-18: Details tab

20. What tunneling protocol is being used?

_____

21. What authentication protocol is being used?

_____

22. What encryption protocol is being used?

_____

23. Click Close.

24. Open a command prompt and execute **ipconfig /all**

25. Why are there multiple IP addresses listed?

_____

_____

26. What are the IP address and default gateway for the remote access connection?

_____

27. How did the computer get that address?

_____

28. Close command prompt.
29. In the **Network Connections** window, right-click **Busicorp via I-net** and choose **Disconnect**.
30. Exit **Network Connections**.

Project 8.6	Comparing WAN Requirements
Overview	An important part of WAN design is the type of connection you plan to use to connect the LANs. By classic definition, a LAN becomes a WAN as soon as data communications cross a public carrier. More companies are using the Internet as their WAN backbone, but this is far from the only connection option. Many established WANs continue to use other connection methods because they do a better job of meeting connection requirements, are more cost-effective, provide a known stable and secure connection, or any combination of the three. You will compare WAN connectivity options during the project.
Outcomes	After completing this project, you will know how to: ▲ identify network categories ▲ identify connection features
What you'll need	To complete this project, you will need: ▲ the following worksheet
Completion time	20 minutes
Precautions	None

■ Part A: Carrier networks

Table 8-1 lists the three WAN network categories. Place each WAN connection type under the appropriate category:

Carrier networks

T-carrier	ATM
PSTN	Frame Relay
X.25	SMDS
POTS	SONET
ISDN	

Table 8-1: WAN network categories

Circuit-switched	Dedicated-circuit	Packet-switched

■ Part B: Carrier service characteristics

Part B includes a table with carrier service types (Table 8-2) and a list of statements that describe one or more of them. Check the boxes for the letters that best describe each access protocol. Each statement applies to at least one carrier. Some statements may apply to multiple carriers.

A. Based on a cloud architecture.
B. Supports bus, ring, and mesh WAN topologies.
C. Uses digital (B) channels and signaling (D) channels.
D. Transmission speeds measured in multiples of OC-1, 51.84 Mbps.
E. Network connections to the carrier are made using a PAD.
F. Could be a dial-up connection to a home phone.
G. Oldest packet-switched service still in use.
H. Have a predictable route over public carriers.
I. Fractional leased circuits are in 65-Kbps multiples.
J. Based on published, generally accepted industry standards.

Table 8-2: Carrier service types

Carrier type	A	B	C	D	E	F	G	H	I	J
PSTN										
ISDN										
SONET										
T-carrier										
ATM										
Frame Relay										
X.25										

9

NETWORK SERVERS AND SERVICES FUNDAMENTALS

PROJECTS

Project 9.1	Understanding Key Concepts
Overview	Part of understanding your options for network configuration is to understand the capabilities of various network operating systems (NOSs). This includes the services they support and how they can be used together in a heterogeneous server environment. Several available NOS options support the same features, functionality, and the same basic network services. When deploying servers in your network, you need to consider interoperability requirements as well as how server placement impacts accessibility and network traffic levels. During this project, you match various server-related terms to the definitions and descriptions of how they are used.
Outcomes	After completing this project, you will know how to: ▲ identify key terms and concepts related to NOS types and versions ▲ identify key terms related to basic network services
What you'll need	To complete this project, you will need: ▲ the worksheet below
Completion time	20 minutes
Precautions	None

The worksheet includes a list of server-related networking terms on the left and descriptions on the right. Match each term with the description that it most closely matches. You will *not* use all descriptions. Each description can be used only once.

___ Shell

___ Mac OS X

___ Linux

___ Kerberos

A. Highly secure industry-standard authentication method. Kerberos was developed for UNIX and is supported on most current NOSs as an authentication method

B. Directory container objects that can contain other objects. These are objects at the mid-levels in a directory structure that are used to contain and organize other objects

C. UNIX/Linux command-line interface

D. Specialized applications that run on web servers and provide services to clients over the Internet

____ Leaf objects

____ Intermediate objects

____ eDirectory

____ Active Directory

____ POSIX

____ Server applications

____ Web services

____ Typefull context

____ Bindery

____ GSNW

E. Shorthand method for describing an object's context or name, but written without labels

F. Microsoft Windows hierarchical directory-based networking, based on X.500 standards

G. Directory object's location, including an object's organization and its OU structure, but not including the object's name

H. Current version of Novell's X.500-based hierarchical network directory service

I. Authentication method used by NetWare servers prior to NetWare 4

J. Operating system designed to look and act exactly like UNIX, but distributed through open source licensing

K. Windows server application that enables a Windows server to act as a gateway giving Windows clients that do not run a NetWare client access to NetWare resources. Supports versions prior to NetWare 5 and IPX/SPX (NWLink) communications only

L. UNIX application development standard

M. Directory objects directly representing directory network entity, such as users and computers

N. Specialized applications that run on server NOSs and provide resources or special services to network clients

O. Macintosh Operating System version built on a UNIX kernel

P. Macintosh operating system version that introduced support for Microsoft's Internet Explorer and for Java Virtual Machine

Project 9.2	Comparing Network Operating Systems
Overview	The most commonly used NOS types and versions are Novell's NetWare and Open Enterprise, Microsoft's Windows Server (most recently Windows Server 2003), UNIX, Linux, and Apple's Macintosh (most recently with OS X). In many ways, these different NOSs are very similar, but they also have striking differences. It is important that you can recognize both the similarities and the differences and use that as part of your basis when selecting an NOS. During this project, you will review various NOS types along with their characteristics and features.
Outcomes	After completing this project, you will know how to: ▲ compare NOS characteristics ▲ compare NOS features
What you'll need	To complete this project, you will need: ▲ the worksheet below
Completion time	20 minutes
Precautions	None

■ Part A: NOS characteristics

Part A includes a table with NOS types (Table 9-1) and a list of statements that describe one or more of them. Check the boxes for the letters that best describe each access protocol. Each statement applies to at least one NOS. Some statements may apply to multiple NOS types.

A. Defaults to TCP/IP as a network protocol.

B. Supports bindery as a downlevel authentication method.

C. Supports NTLM as a downlevel authentication method.

D. Provides a user interface for running standard applications.

E. Deployed as a dedicated server.

F. Based on or emulates a UNIX kernel.

G. Uses a directory system to locate network objects and resources.

H. Can be downloaded, deployed, and used at no charge.

Table 9-1: NOS types

NOS	A	B	C	D	E	F	G	H
Novell Netware/Open Enterprise								
Windows Server 2003								
UNIX								
Linux								
Mac OS X								

■ Part B: NOS features

Part B includes a table with NOS types (Table 9-2) and a list of features. Check the boxes for the letters that best describe each NOS. Each statement applies to exactly one NOS.

A. Uses Samba to support Windows clients.

B. Uses the Open Directory system.

C. Includes NWLink protocol support.

D. Provides a management interface only.

E. Uses X Windows as GUI user interface.

F. Saves documents in PDF format as native file format.

G. Runs on SUSe Linux.

H. Native requests for services use SMB protocol requests.

I. Native support for printers and printer management uses LPD/LPR protocols.

J. Includes Keychain for password storage.

Table 9-2: NOS features

NOS	A	B	C	D	E	F	G	H	I	J
Novell Open Enterprise										
Windows Server 2003										
UNIX/Linux										
Mac OS X										

Project 9.3	Understanding Basic Services
Overview	All of the NOSs in common use support a variety of basic services. That means that many of your network's requirements can be met without having to purchase additional server applications. In some cases, you can even configure a server to support multiple services, cutting down on your hardware requirements. One common example is having a server act as both a file and print server.
	The specific services supported depend on the NOS. All of those in common use support file and print services and can be configured to support some kind of user authentication. It's common to see web server support included as well. Some, like most Linux distributions, include more specialized service, such as database services, while others require you to purchase separate server applications for that purpose. Some services are provided as a feature of the TCP/IP protocol. These include DNS and DHCP services.
	In this project, you will review some key points about basic services and look at some options for setting up servers to support various basic services.
Outcomes	After completing this project, you will know how to: ▲ identify how basic server types are used ▲ explain options for configuring Windows Server 2003 roles ▲ explain how to configure a Windows XP peer print server
What you'll need	To complete this project, you will need: ▲ a computer running Windows Server 2003 ▲ a computer running Widows XP ▲ the workshcct below
Completion time	45 minutes
Precautions	The instructions in this project assume you are working on a two-node network with one computer running Windows XP Professional and one computer running Windows Server 2003. If these computers are part of a larger classroom network, your instructor will provide you with alternate instructions for configuring network and domain parameters.
	If working on an existing network, you must review the project steps with your network administrator. Your network administrator may need to make changes or additions to the instructions.

■ Part A: Basic services

In this part of the project, you are asked a series of questions about services that you will commonly find on most LANs.

1. What is the general guideline for physical placement of file and print servers in a routed network?

    _____

    _____

2. Why?

    _____

    _____

3. The Kerberos protocol is most commonly associated with servers acting in what role?

    _____

4. Why do some NOSs include other protocols that are used in the same role (include at least one example)?

    _____

    _____

    _____

    _____

5. In a TCP/IP network, when would you need to deploy DNS servers?

    _____

    _____

    _____

    _____

6. When would you need to deploy DHCP servers?

    _____

    _____

7. When would you need to deploy servers configured as routers?

_____

_____

_____

8. What kind of server would you most commonly find deployed outside of your internal network, separated from the network by a firewall?

_____

9. Why?

_____

_____

10. When would you include a NAT server on your network?

_____

_____

_____

■ Part B: View available service configurations

In this part of the project, you will view some of the service configurations and roles supported by Windows Server 2003. Currently, your Windows Server 2003 computer is configured as an Active Directory domain controller, but the operating system is designed to support a wide range of optional services as server roles. You should be logged on as an Administrator at the start of the part of the project.

1. If **Manage Your Server** is not already open on your desktop, open the **Start** menu, point to **Administrative Tools**, and select **Manage Your Server**.
2. Click **Add or remove a role**, as indicated in Figure 9-1.

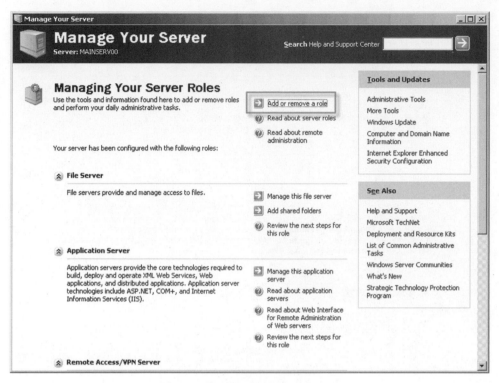

Figure 9-1: Manage Your Server

3. Click Next.

4. What roles is your server currently configured to support?

_____

_____

5. Click **Configure Your Server Log**. This displays information about when each of the roles was configured.

6. Close the configuration log.

7. According to the **Server Role** dialog box, what should you use to configure a role that isn't listed?

_____

Note: In the next several steps, you will remove the remote access server role. If the computer is not configured as a remote access server, skip steps 8 through 11 and continue with step 12.

8. Click **Remote access/VPN server** and click Next.

Note: This as the same effect as disabling the RRAS server in the Routing and Remote Access console.

9. Check **Remove the remote access/VPN server role**, as shown in Figure 9-2, and click Next.

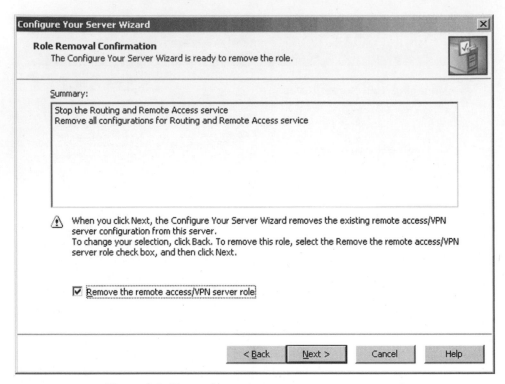

Figure 9-2: Removing remote access server support

10. When prompted to verify your action, click Yes.

11. Click Finish when prompted.

12. Open the **Start** menu, select **Control Panel**, and then select **Add or Remove Programs**.

13. Click **Add/Remove Windows Components**. This is a second way of configuring services and roles.

14. Scroll through the list and view the other services available.

15. Select **Other Network File and Print Services** and click Details.

16. This lists available services. Check **Print Services for Macintosh** and **Print Services for Unix**, as shown in Figure 9-3.

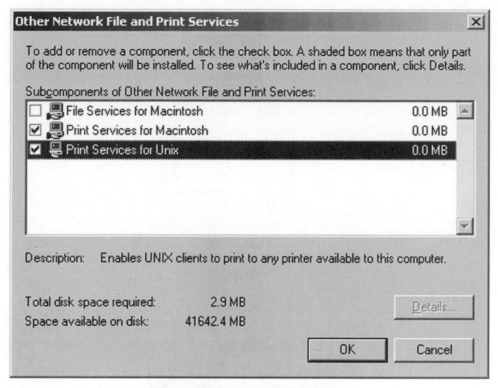

Figure 9-3: Print services selected

17. Click OK.

18. Click Next. If prompted, insert the Windows Server 2003 installation CD.

19. Click Finish when prompted.

20. Exit **Add or Remove Programs**.

21. What is the potential security concern when configuring multiple service support?

_____

_____

22. What is the potential performance concern?

_____

_____

_____

23 The **Services** utility gives you a way to temporarily stop a service. This might be necessary, for example, when troubleshooting a performance problem. Open the Start menu, point to **Administrative Tools**, and select **Services**.

24. Scroll down and then locate and select **TCP/IP Print Server**, as shown in Figure 9-4. You enabled this server when you installed UNIX printer support.

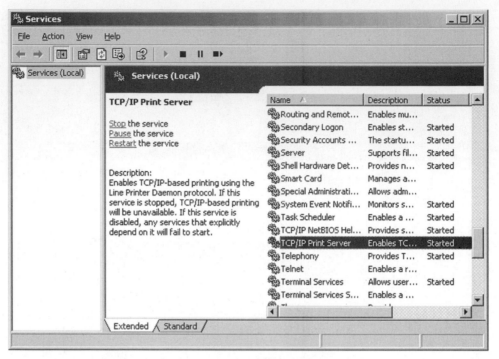

Figure 9-4: TCP/IP Print Server

25. Double-click **TCP/IP Print Server** to open its **Properties** dialog box and click Stop. This will stop the service until manually restarted or until the computer is restarted.

26. Click OK and then exit **Services**.

■ Part C: Configure a peer server

You will complete this part of the project on the computer running Windows XP. Peer servers, which are computers that act as both network clients and servers, are common on Windows, UNIX, Linux, and Macintosh networks. You will also sometimes see Windows servers used as peer servers on a Novell network. During this part of the project, you will configure the computer running Windows XP as a peer print server, a commonly used configuration.

This project assumes that you do not have a printer configured on the computer. This project also assumes that you have the **Control Panel** configured in **Classic View**.

1. Open the **Start** menu and select the **Control Panel**.

2. Double-click **Printers and Faxes**.

3. Click **Add a printer**, as indicated in Figure 9-5.

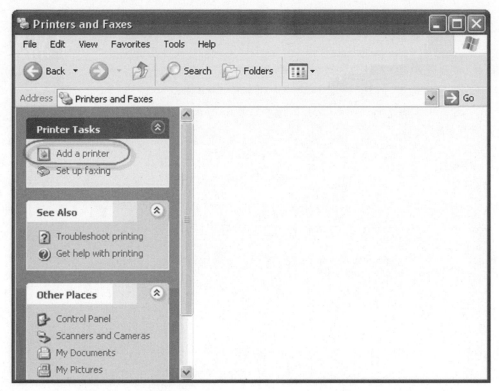

Figure 9-5: Printers and Faxes window

4. Click Next.

5. Remove the check from **Automatically detect and install my Plug and Play printer**, as in Figure 9-6, and then click Next.

Figure 9-6: Manually selecting a printer

6. Leave the port at default **(LTP1)** and click Next.

7. Under **Manufacturer**, select **HP** and under **Model**, select **LaserJet 4 Plus** (see Figure 9-7), and then click Next.

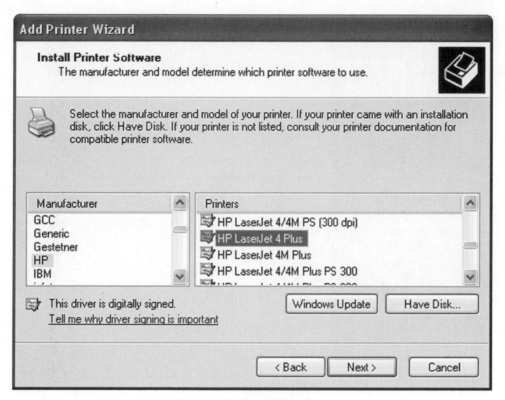

Figure 9-7: Selected printer

8. Change the printer name to **SharedHP** and click Next.

9. You make the computer a print server by sharing the printer. Select **Share name**, leave the name at default, and click Next.

10. The **Location and Comment** are optional fields and are provided so you can enter information about the printer, such as its physical location in the office. Leave these fields blank and click Next.

11. When prompted to print a text page, select **No** and then click Next.

12. Why shouldn't you print a test page to this printer?

    _____

    _____

13. Review the summary information, which should look like Figure 9-8, and click Finish to install the printer.

Figure 9-8: Completed printer configuration

14. You should see the printer listed like the example shown in Figure 9-9 when installation is complete.

Figure 9-9: Installed printer

15. Right-click **SharedHP** and select **Properties**.
16. Select the **Sharing** tab, as shown in Figure 9-10.

Figure 9-10: Printer sharing properties

17. The **List in the directory** property is available only because the computer is an Active Directory domain member. This causes the printer to be listed as a resource in the Active Directory. Click OK to close the **Properties** dialog box and then close the **Printers and Faxes** window.

■ Part D: Verify a resource listing

You will complete this part of the project on the computer running Windows Server 2003. You will verify that the printer is listed in and available through the Active Directory.

1. Open the **Start** menu and select **Printers and Faxes**.
2. Double-click **Add printer** to open the **Add Printer Wizard**.
3. Click Next.
4. Select **A network printer, or a printer attached to another computer** and then click Next.
5. Leave **Find a printer in the directory selected** (the default selection) and click Next.
6. Leave the prompts at default and click Find Now. You should see the printer listed, as shown in Figure 9-11.

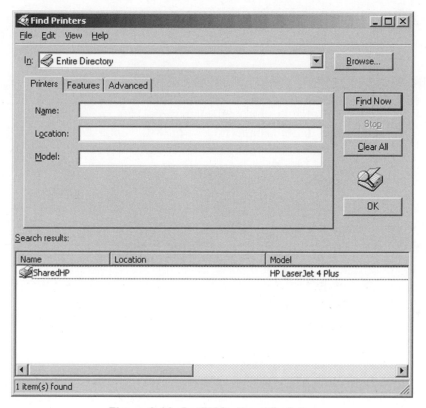

Figure 9-11: Available shared printer

7. Select **SharedHP** and click OK.

8. Click Next.

9. Click Finish.

10. The printer is now listed in **Printers and Faxes**, as shown in Figure 9-12.

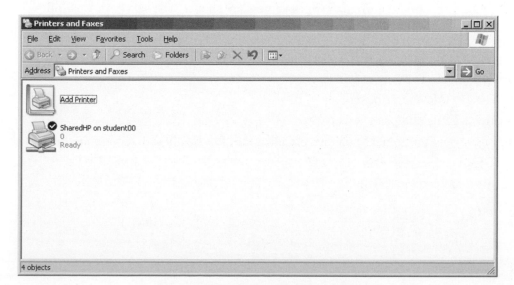

Figure 9-12: Installed shared printer

11. Close **Printers and Faxes**.

Project 9.4	Determining Server Placement
Overview	Windows XP Professional can be configured to support both incoming and outgoing dial-up connections. You will want to be cautious when configuring an incoming dial-up connection because it is an entry point to your computer from anywhere with a phone line. This is particularly true if your computer is connected to a network. In this project you will identify where to place various servers to meet network design requirements.
Outcomes	After completing this project, you will know how to: ▲ identify the impact of server placement in various scenarios ▲ find ways to avoid or minimize network problems
What you'll need	To complete this project, you will need: ▲ the worksheet below
Completion time	30 minutes
Precautions	None

■ Part A: LAN configuration

The questions in Part A refer to the configuration shown in Figure 9-13. The network is a routed TCP/IP LAN. Some of the current network servers are shown. The servers are as follows:

- Serv1—Domain controller
- Serv2—Domain controller and DNS
- Serv3—Domain controller
- Gen1—File and print server
- Gen2—File and print server

Figure 9.13 shows the logical network organization. Physically, all servers are kept in the same secure room. The network supports approximately 90 hosts, including servers.

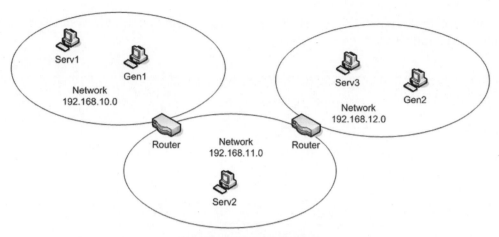

Figure 9-13: Routed LAN

1. The network was configured as a routed LAN without completely considering network requirements. You are considering to combine the subnetworks. What is the main network characteristic that you must consider before doing this and why?

   _____

   _____

2. Other than removing the routers and physically connecting the central connection devices, what would the change require?

   _____

   _____

3. What is the most likely impact on the network if Serv3 fails?

   _____

   _____

   _____

   _____

4. What is the most likely impact on the network if Serv2 fails?

   _____

   _____

   _____

5. How can you minimize the potential problems?

   _____

   _____

6. If you were deploying a single DHCP server for the network, where would you place it to minimize overall network traffic and why?

    _____

    _____

    _____

    _____

7. What if you were deploying two DHCP servers?

    _____

    _____

    _____

    _____

■ Part B: Demand-dial configuration

The questions in Part B refer to the configuration shown in Figure 9-14. The network is a routed TCP/IP LAN. It is also configured as a Windows Active Directory network. Some of the current network servers are shown. The servers shown are as follows:

- Serv1—Demand-dial router
- Serv2—Demand-dial router
- Serv3—Demand-dial router

Currently, connections between each subnet are made over the public-switched telephone network (PSTN) using dial-up modems. Each server is configured with one modem. Access permissions are configured so that access to print and file servers is limited to hosts on the same subnet.

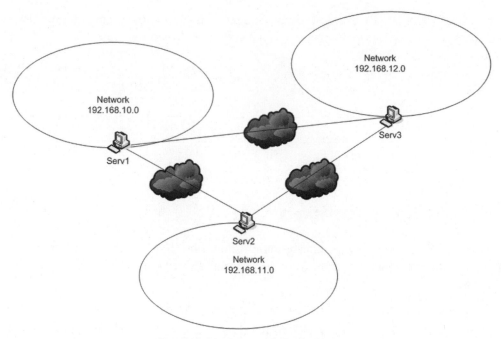

Figure 9-14: Demand-dial network

1. What are the biggest concerns in relation to communication between subnets?

_____

_____

_____

2. Domain controllers will also be configured as DNS servers. You are planning to deploy a domain controller in each subnet. Justify this decision.

_____

_____

_____

3. What traffic will be required between the subnets?

_____

_____

_____

4. Each subnet's NetBIOS name resolution requirements are for the local subnet only. What do you need to do to support name resolution while keeping traffic and administrative requirements to a minimum?

_____

_____

_____

■ Part C: Heterogeneous network

The questions in Part C refer to the configuration shown in Figure 9-15. The network is a routed TCP/IP LAN. Some of the current network servers and clients are shown. The computers shown are as follows:

- Linux1—Linux file server also used as a user workstation
- Mac1—Mac OS X computer used primarily as a graphics and multimedia file server
- Mac2—Mac OS X client used for commercial art and high-resolution graphics
- Mac3—Mac OS X client used for commercial art, movies, and high-resolution graphics
- Serv1—Windows Server 2003 file, print, and intranet web server
- Serv2—Windows Server 2003 database server
- Serv3—Windows 2000 Server print server with high-resolution graphics printer

The majority of the client computers run Windows XP or Windows 2000 Professional. There are also a few Linux workstations used as client computers. The only computers that need access to Mac1 are Mac2 and Mac3. Mac2 and Mac3 also need to access Serv1. The Macintosh computers print both draft and final copies of graphics files to the printer connected to Serv3. Client computers access Serv2 using various custom database applications. All clients need access to Serv2. Linux1 supports Windows and Linux clients only.

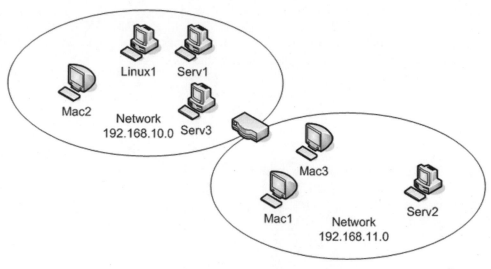

Figure 9-15: Heterogeneous network

1. In order to minimize administrative overhead, what should you use as the primary NOS for this network?

   _____

2. Why?

   _____

   _____

   _____

3. What would be necessary for Linux1 to provide the necessary client support?

   _____

4. Why?

   _____

5. What authentication protocol would be used, based on your proposed configuration? Explain your answer.

   _____

6. What other authentication protocols, if any, would be needed?

   _____

   _____

7. Of the computers shown in Figure 9-15, what changes could you make to computer placement to reduce the traffic through the router and why?

_____

_____

_____

8. How would this affect the placement of Serv2, if at all?

_____

_____

_____

Project 9.5	Observing Network Traffic Flows
Overview	One of the determining factors in server placement is how servers impact traffic flows and bandwidth requirements. Different NOS products provide various tools for monitoring network traffic and collecting this information. There are also third-party tools designed specifically for network monitoring. It is generally suggested that you collect baseline performance information when you first deploy the network. It's best to collect this information at various times so you have an idea of peak, minimum, and average network traffic levels. You would then check network traffic periodically or any time a communication problem related to traffic levels is suspected. During this project, you will monitor the traffic generated by sample activities.
Outcomes	After completing this project, you will know how to: ▲ observe traffic using Network Monitor ▲ observe performance using System Monitor
What you'll need	To complete this project, you will need: ▲ domain controller running Windows Server 2003 ▲ domain member running Windows XP Professional ▲ the worksheet below
Completion time	30 minutes
Precautions	The instructions in this project assume you are working on a two-node network with one computer running Windows XP Professional and one computer running Windows Server 2003. If these computers are part of a larger classroom network, your instructor will provide you with alternate instructions for configuring network and domain parameters. If working on an existing network, you must review the project steps with your network administrator. Your network administrator may need to make changes or additions to the instructions. Watch the project instructions carefully. You will be using both computers throughout this project.

■ Part A: View logon traffic

Log on can generate significant traffic on a network and place a noticeable load on the authenticating server, depending on the number of clients involved. During this part of the project you see the load generated when one user logs on.

1. Shut down the computer running Windows XP.

2. On the computer running Windows Server 2003, open the **Start** menu, point to **Administrative Tools**, and select **Performance** to launch the **Performance** utility with **System Monitor** selected, as shown in Figure 9-16.

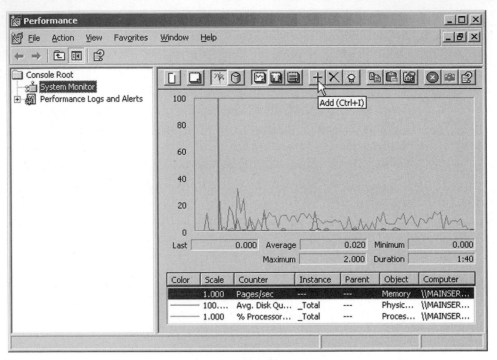

Figure 9-16: System Monitor

3. By default, **System Monitor** is watching selected local resources only. Click the Add toolbar icon (+ sign), indicated in Figure 9-16.

   Note: You may find it easier to view monitored traffic if you remove the default counters. To do so, select the counter that you want to remove and press Del or click the Delete toolbar icon.

4. Select **Network Interface** as the **Performance Object**, **Bytes Total/sec** under **Select counters from list**, and your network adapter (see Figure 9-17). Click Add.

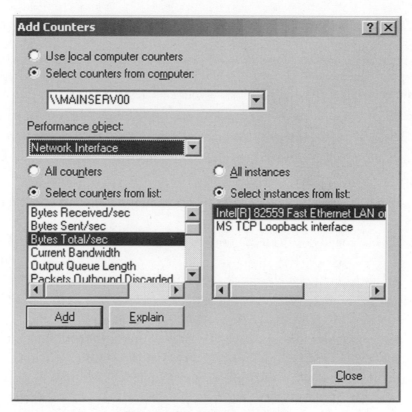

Figure 9-17: Adding counters

5. Select **Current Bandwidth** under **Select counters from list** and click Add. Click Close.

6. Right-click the area where the counters are listed and select **Properties**.

7. Select the **Graph** tab to set the graph scale, set **Maximum value** to **10**, and then click OK. This is necessary to see the relatively small bandwidth and traffic changes that will occur. Periodically check **System Monitor** through the project to see how your actions impact the performance counters.

8. Open the **Start** menu, point to **Administrative Tools**, and select **Network Monitor**. If prompted to select a network, select your local network connection.

9. Select **Capture** and then **Start**.

10. Restart the computer running Windows XP. Observe **Network Monitor** and **System Monitor** while the computer restarts.

11. Select **Capture** and then **Stop** in **Network Monitor**.

12. Select **Capture** and then **Start**. Do not save the capture when prompted.

13. Log on from your computer running Windows XP.

14. Select **Capture** and then **Stop and View**. Scroll through the traffic. Notice the volume of traffic generated by a single computer's log on.

15. Do not exit **System Monitor** or **Network Monitor**.

■ Part B: View name resolution traffic

1. On the computer running Windows XP, open the **TCP/IP Protocol Properties** dialog box and verify that your domain controller is configured as the primary DNS server. If not, enter your domain controllers IP address and save your changes.

2. Open the **Start** menu, point to **All Programs** and then to **Accessories**, and select **Notepad**.

3. Open the following file in **Notepad**: **\Windows\System32\Drivers\Etc\Hosts**

4. If there is an entry for your domain controller, delete that entry and save your changes.

5. Exit **Notepad**.

6. On the computer running Windows XP, open a command prompt and execute **ipconfig /flushdns**

7. What does this command do? (You can run **ipconfig /?** for help.)

_____

8. On the computer running Windows Server 2003, close the traffic window and select **Capture** and then **Start**. Do not save the capture when prompted.

9. On the computer running Windows XP, execute **ping mainserv00.busicorp.com** and then switch quickly back to the computer running Windows Server 2003.

10. Select **Capture** and then **Stop and View**. You should see DNS traffic, as shown in Figure 9-18.

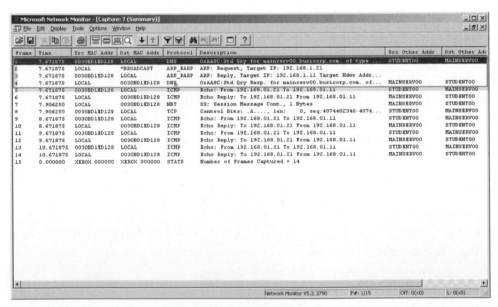

Figure 9-18: Captured traffic

The ICMP traffic was generated by the ping command.

11. Repeat steps 8 through 10. Do you see a difference in the DNS traffic generated?

_____

12. What caused this?

_____

_____

13. How could you test to verify this?

_____

_____

14. Test your theory to see if you were correct.

15. Start a capture and let it run for a while to capture background network traffic. Stop and view after a few minutes. It may take a few minutes before you detect any traffic. This is the type of activity going on across the network even when "nothing" is happening. Scroll through and see what protocols, if any, you recognize. Background activity will vary somewhat between different networks, depending on what other computers and services, if any, are running on the network.

16. On both computers, close all open windows.

17. During these tests, the performance indicated for **Network Interface** in **System Monitor** should have been minimal. Considering that, why might these types of traffic be a concern in a live network?

_____

_____

_____

10

WIDE AREA AND ENTERPRISE NETWORKING SERVICES

PROJECTS

Project 10.1	Understanding Key Concepts
Overview	As companies grow, so do their networks. That means that just because you're responsible for a LAN today, that doesn't mean that you won't be managing a WAN tomorrow, or at least some time in the near future. This also means that network design, for most networks, is no longer a task you do once and forget. If you are preparing to work with enterprise networks, you need to understand the terminology related to those networks. Many of these terms apply to both LAN and WAN environments. During this project, you will match various management-related terms to the definitions and descriptions of how they are used.
Outcomes	After completing this project, you will know how to: ▲ identify key terms and concepts related to WANs and network design
What you'll need	To complete this project, you will need: ▲ the worksheet below
Completion time	20 minutes
Precautions	None

The worksheet includes a list of management-related networking terms on the left and descriptions on the right. Match each term with the description that it most closely matches. You will *not* use all descriptions. Each description can be used only once.

____   Capacity planning

____   Circuit loading

____   Local loop circuit

____   Upstream circuit

A. Network technology closest to the user, typically the LAN or remote access connection

B. Network design process based on lengthy, detailed analysis and often taking up to 2 years to complete the design

C. Network design process based on the concept that networks that use a few standard components are less expensive in the long run than networks that use a wide variety of components

D. Process of estimating the size and type of network circuits needed

___ Downstream circuit

E. Place at which an ISP provides services to its customers (the customers' connections to the ISP)

___ Access layer

F. Innermost part of the network connecting distribution layer networks, as with WAN connections

___ Distribution layer

G. Result of the technology design process, identifying the network hardware and software needed, typically as design diagrams

___ Core layer

H. Term referring to the amount of traffic that a circuit must carry

___ Building-block process

I. Circuit design in which several customers connect to the same circuit, sharing the available bandwidth

___ Turnpike effect

J. Part of the network that connects the access layer to the rest of the network as with a backbone network

___ Shared multipoint circuit

K. Term referring to traffic from the carrier or ISP to the customer

___ Physical network design

L. Goal of the needs assessment design phase, consisting of a statement of the required network elements

___ Logical network design

M. Term referring to the circuit carrying traffic from the customer to the carrier or ISP

___ POP

N. When network use exceeds original estimates simply because the network and its services are available to the users

___ ARP

O. TCP/IP protocol that resolves a device's IP address from its MAC address

P. The connection between the carrier's central office and the customer

Q. TCP/IP protocol that resolves a device's MAC address from its IP address

Project 10.2	Identifying Network Design Requirements
Overview	The network design process is usually treated as a series of design phases. Often, these are broken down into needs analysis, technology design, and cost assessment. However, neither of these phases is completely isolated. Each impacts the other, and during the design process you often have to go back and forth between the design phases until you are finished.
	It's important to understand the design process, including the design phases, and what you should do during each phase. You also need to know the expected deliverable for each phase.
	This project focuses on network design phases, including the requirements of each and expected deliverables.
Outcomes	After completing this project, you will know how to:
	▲ identify network design phases
	▲ identify design phase deliverables
What you'll need	To complete this project, you will need:
	▲ the worksheet below
Completion time	30 minutes
Precautions	None

■ Part A: Design phases

Part A includes a table with the network design phases (Table 10-1) and a list of statements that describe one or more of them. Check the boxes for the letters that best describe each design phase. Each statement applies to at least one design phase. Some statements may apply to multiple design phases.

A. Deliverables include a set of network diagrams.

B. Product brands and models are determined.

C. Product vendors are identified.

D. Router placement is determined.

E. Includes identification of the access, distribution, and core layers.

F. Includes determining circuit loading.

G. RFP is one of the deliverables.

H. Requirements are organized as mandatory, desireable, and wish list.

I. Includes identification of application servers.

J. Sometimes uses network discovery tools and simulations.

Table 10-1: Network design phases

Design phase	A	B	C	D	E	F	G	H	I	J
Needs analysis										
Technology design										
Cost assessment										

■ Part B: Network design

Part A includes a table with the network and a logical network diagram (Figure 10-1). Match each labeled area on the network diagram with the geographic scope layer in Table 10-2. Each letter applies to one and only one layer.

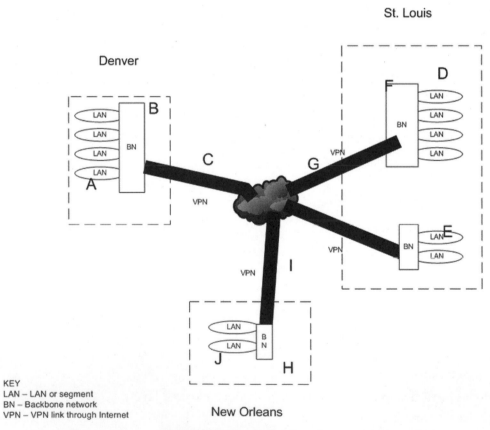

Figure 10-1: Logical network

Table 10-2: Network layers

Network layer	A	B	C	D	E	F	G	H	I	J
Access										
Distribution										
Core										

■ Part C: Physical network design

Part A includes a table with the network and a physical network diagram (Figure 10-2). This is a detailed diagram of the Denver LAN based on the logical network diagram shown in Figure 10-1. The network connects to other networks through a VPN link through the Internet. There is also a connection to the public Internet for client access and to support public web servers. LAN traffic needs to support a circuit load of up to 100 Mbps.

Match each labeled area on the network diagram with the appropriate network hardware. One or more devices of that type could be installed at each labeled area. A letter can apply to more than one type of hardware. Some types of hardware may not be used.

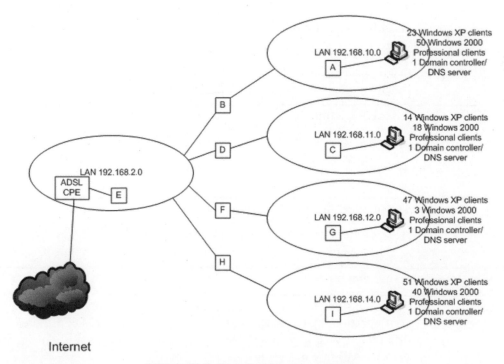

Figure 10-2: Physical Denver network

Network layer	A	B	C	D	E	F	G	H	I
Hub									
Switch									
Bridge									
Router									
RRAS Server									

Project 10.3	Designing a Network
Overview	The network design process includes careful analysis and detailed network design. Several design decisions must be made along the way. Sometimes it will be necessary to rethink some of your decisions later in the process when conditions change or you discover additional information. When dealing with an existing network, a key part of the process is completing your network inventory. You need to identify the computers (clients and servers) that are on the network and information about each. There are automated tools to assist with the process, but other tools like checklists can also be helpful. This project has you go through selected network design activities in some detail. This includes information gathering and making design decisions based on what you know about the network.
Outcomes	After completing this project, you will know how to: ▲ inventory network resources ▲ identify and rank network resources ▲ identify network devices
What you'll need	To complete this project, you will need: ▲ a computer running Windows Server 2003 ▲ this worksheet
Completion time	30 minutes
Precautions	There are some assumptions made in this project as to your server's configuration, based on earlier projects. If your server is configured differently, your answers will vary. This does not necessarily mean that your answers are incorrect.

■ Part A: Computer inventory

In this part of the project, you will inventory your domain controller. You should be logged on as an Administrator at the beginning of this project. This part of the project includes a computer inventory worksheet. As you work through the project steps, complete the worksheet.

Computer name: _____

Operating system: _____

Server roles: _____

IP address: _____

Primary DNS: _____

WINS: _____

NIC make and model: _____

Video adapter: _____

■ Part B: Identify network requirements

In this part of the project, you will answer questions related to network design decisions. Refer to Figure 10-3 for this project.

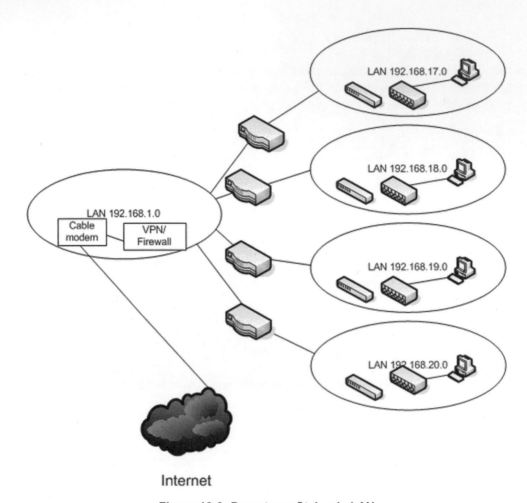

Figure 10-3: Downtown St. Louis LAN

Busicorp has one office location in downtown St. Louis. The office connects to the WAN via VPN connections over the Internet. There are no plans at this time to modify the downtown LAN. You will be deploying the West County areas of St. Louis County after you complete the network design. Both LANs will be part of the same Windows Active Directory domain.

In the existing network, you have a domain controller that is also configured as a DNS server in each subnet. You have a DHCP server in network 192.168.17.0 that also supports network 192.168.18.0 and a DHCP server in network 192.168.19.0 that also supports network 192.168.20.0.

Details of the West County LAN are as follows:

- Thirty initial clients evenly spread between two subnets with planned growth to 30 or more in each.
- Two private subnets (192.168.21.0 and 192.168.22.0) connected to a 100-Mbps backbone (192.168.5.0).
- Design must include network hardware except cable plant, which will be handled by building facilities.
- A separate connection will provide Internet connectivity for client computers.

- Initial servers must include domain controllers, DNS servers, a file/print server, and internal web server.

Clients will receive their addresses through DHCP. You need to be able to establish eight collision domains on the new LAN to cover communication requirements as the office grows. Hardware costs should be kept to a minimum.

You are not responsible for the wide area connection or any of its related hardware. That will be handled separately by a different design group. The wide area link will connect to your backbone.

1. What servers must you include as mandatory requirements in the new LAN?

   _____

2. What servers should you include as desired requirements, if any (explain why)?

   _____

   _____

3. Assuming you are directed to deploy no more than three physical servers, how should you configure them to meet the mandatory requirements?

   _____

   _____

4. Explain your reasoning for the server configurations.

   _____

   _____

   _____

   _____

5. You want to deploy a WAP/router with one public-side connector for the cable modem and four private-side connectors on LAN 192.168.21.0. It supports client network address translation and has a built-in firewall. What are the advantages, if any, of using this device?

   _____

   _____

   _____

6. What are the potential disadvantages?

   _____

   _____

   _____

7. Describe how it would be connected to the network.

_____

_____

_____

8. Add a sketch of the new LAN to Figure 10-3. Do not include the servers, just connection devices.

■ Part C: Identify network hardware

Part C uses the same LAN segments as Part B. Base your answers on your physical network design in Part B.

The company's purchase guidelines call for using routers with two NICs installed, 8-port switches, and 16-port hubs in all network designs.

1. How many access layer segments are present in your new design (old and new LANs) and what are they?

_____

_____

_____

2. Distribution layer?

_____

3. Core layer?

_____

4. How many of each of the following will you need for your initial deployment. Explain your answers:

   a. Switches

   _____

   b. Hubs

   _____

   c. Routers

   _____

5. What fault tolerance for network services, if any, is built into your server deployment design?

_____

_____

6. What would be the advantage of purchasing all client computers with the same hardware configuration?

_____

_____

Project 10.4	Researching Network Hardware
Overview	During the technical design phase you work on creating the network's physical network design. During this process you identify the network devices that you need and determine their placement. That includes ensuring that the equipment can support the projected circuit load. Often overlapping this process is cost assessment. During this phase, you identify the potential vendors and then have them provide cost estimates. Technical design and cost assessment often overlap. You might choose to adjust your physical design based on hardware availability and cost. During this project you will research network hardware availability from three online vendors.
Outcomes	After completing this project, you will know how to: ▲ research hardware cost and availability ▲ estimate network hardware cost
What you'll need	To complete this project, you will need: ▲ a computer with Internet access ▲ to first complete Project 10.3 ▲ this worksheet
Completion time	30 minutes
Precautions	The retailers chosen for this project were chosen because they are representative of their type of business, have a presence throughout the United States, and are accessible through their websites. It should not be taken as an endorsement or recommendation of these retailers or their products. Your instructor may choose to have you research different retailers during this project. If working on an existing network, you must review the project steps with your network administrator. Your network administrator may need to make changes or additions to the instructions.

During this project you will research hardware availability and cost from three vendors. These are:

- Office Depot: www.officedepot.com
- Amazon: www.amazon.com
- CDW: www.cdw.com

Office Depot is a traditional "brick-and-mortar" retailer that also has a online retail presence. Office Depot is a general office supply retailer that, in recent years, has branched out to include computer hardware and other office-related consumer electronics.

Amazon started out as an online bookseller, but has become the Web's most popular one-stop shop. Its product mix includes both consumer electronics and a wide variety of computer and network hardware.

CDW does business under a variety of names, including PC Warehouse, MacWarehouse, and Warehouse.com. Its primary business is computer and network hardware and software. It focuses on supporting small-to-large business customers.

For each of the devices, if the vendor does not offer a device of that type or you can't find the information requested, enter "N/A."

■ Part A: Hub

In Part A, research each of the retailer sites, find the hubs offered for sale, and complete the Table 10-3.

Table 10-3: Hubs

Feature	Office Depot	Amazon	CDW
Make/model			
Price			
Speed			
Supported standards			

■ Part B: Switches

In Part B, research each of the retailer sites, find the switches offered for sale, and complete Table 10-4.

Table 10-4: Switches

Feature	Office Depot	Amazon	CDW
Make/model			
Price			
Speed			
Supported standards			

■ Part C: WAP/broadband routers

In Part C, research each of the retailer sites, find the broadband DSL-cable modem/wireless routers offered for sale, and complete Table 10-5.

Table 10-5: WAP/broadband routers

Feature	Office Depot	Amazon	CDW
Make/model			
Price			
Wired speed			
Wired ports			
Hub/switch?			
Supported standards			

■ Part D: Routers

In Part D, research each of the retailer sites, find the wired routers offered for sale, and complete Table 10-6. You are looking for wired routers only. Do not include wireless routers.

Table 10-6: Routers

Feature	Office Depot	Amazon	CDW
Make/model			
Price			
Number of ports			
Relevant features			

■ Part E: Cost estimates

Complete Table 10-7 based on your equipment estimates from Project 10.3 and cost estimates from this project. Use the best price you found for each item. If the best price you found for switches is better than the best price for hubs, feel free to substitute switches for hubs. Do not consider any costs other than the hardware price in this table. After completing the table, answer the questions that follow.

Table 10-7: Cost estimates

Equipment	Number required	Cost for each	Total cost
Hub			
Switch			
WAP			
Router			

1. What is the total hardware cost?

    _____

2. What network hardware is not included in this estimate?

    _____

3. What other costs might you need to consider when ordering the hardware?

    _____

4. Some businesses assign a specific salesperson to your account after you register as a customer. What are potential benefits of this?

    _____

    _____

5. What are potential drawbacks?

    _____

    _____

Project 10.5	Investigating Service Options
Overview	Internet connection options have expanded in recent years. DSL and cable Internet providers have shifted their focus from home consumers to business customers. The bandwidths supported by their connection options more than meet the needs of most small- to medium-sized businesses. Some also offer services targeted at large businesses and enterprise networks, including business-specific services such as static IP addresses, VPN connections, and so on. During this project, you will research the service offerings of two high-speed Internet ISPs.
Outcomes	After completing this project, you will know how to: ▲ configure a VPN connection
What you'll need	To complete this project, you will need: ▲ a computer with Internet access ▲ this worksheet
Completion time	30 minutes
Precautions	Internet access is required to complete this project. The completion time will vary depending on various factors, such as connection speed and how long it takes you to navigate the provider's website. Specific navigation hints have not been given because the sample providers frequently update and modify their websites. Selection of the service providers used in the project should not be taken as an endorsement or recommendation of these providers or their services. Your instructor may choose to have you research different providers during this project.

You will be researching two high-speed Internet service providers, comparing prices for DSL business services provided by EarthLink and high-speed cable business services provided by Charter Communications. Your instructor may have you use different service providers. The website URLs are:

- EarthLink: www.earthlink.com
- Charter Communications: www.charter.com

You will need to navigate through each of the websites to locate the information you need. Look for connection rates between 3 and 5 Mbps (preferably 5 Mbps). Focus your search on business services provided by each of the ISPs. Because companies often change their websites to keep the content fresh, the project does not provide any navigation hints. However, business service links are clearly identified on both providers' websites and both include a search function to let you search for specific services.

If you are prompted for address information at any point, use the following, or another address provided by your instructor:

Street address: 100 Main

ZIP: 63601

If you are unable to find an answer, write "Could not find" in the space.

■ Part A: DSL service

EarthLink is an ISP company that provides an array of services. Traditionally, it provided dial-up telephone service only, but has added support for ISDN, DSL, and even fiber optic WAN connections. Visit the EarthLink website and answer the following questions regarding the support for small- to medium-sized businesses:

1. What is the cost per month?

   _____

2. What is the access speed (download/upload)?

   _____

3. Is the line speed guaranteed?

   _____

4. How many static IP addresses, if any, are provided?

   _____

5. How many e-mail accounts are provided?

   _____

6. How much space per mailbox is provided?

   _____

7. What is the access technology?

   _____

8. Do they support VPNs?

   _____

9. Do they support web servers?

   _____

10. Do they support SSL?

   _____

■ Part B: Cable modem service

Charter Communications is one of the largest cable television providers in the U.S. In recent years it has added support for high-speed Internet access and voice over IP (VoIP) telephone service. It has business service options designed to meet the needs of various sized businesses. Visit the Charter website and answer the following questions regarding their support for small- to medium-sized businesses.

1. What is the cost per month?

   _____

2. What is the access speed (download/upload)?

   _____

3. Is the line speed guaranteed?

   _____

4. How many static IP addresses, if any, are provided?

   _____

5. How many e-mail accounts are provided?

   _____

6. How much web space is provided?

   _____

7. Do they support VPN?

   _____

8. Do they support web hosting?

   _____

11

NETWORK MANAGEMENT

Project 11.1	Understanding Key Concepts
Overview	Understanding the management process means, in part, understanding terms related to the management process. It's also important that you understand the tools and technologies available to you to help with the management process. During this project, you match various management-related terms to the definitions and descriptions of how they are used.
Outcomes	After completing this project, you will know how to: ▲ identify key terms and concepts related to network management
What you'll need	To complete this project, you will need: ▲ the worksheet below
Completion time	20 minutes
Precautions	None

The worksheet includes a list of management-related networking terms on the left and descriptions on the right. Match each term with the description that it most closely matches. You will *not* use all descriptions. Each description can be used only once.

____ SMS

____ Full backup

____ Incremental backup

____ Differential backup

____ Disk mirroring

____ Disk striping with parity

____ MIB

A. Referring to a device that can be replaced without powering off

B. RAID 1 disk fault tolerant configuration using two hard disks with identical data connected to a single disk controller

C. Disk operations waiting to be processed

D. Microsoft's SNMP-based network management system

E. All management information objects on a network

F. Emerging ESD software standard

G. RAID 1 disk fault tolerant configuration using two hard disks with identical data connected to a separate disk controller

____ Threshold

____ NOC

____ Hot-swappable

____ Disk queue

____ ESD

____ Automatic failover

____ Manual failover

H. Switch between a primary and a redundant server that does not require administrator or operator intervention

I. Backup in which only changed files are backed up and the archive bit is not changed

J. Backup in which only changed files are backed up and the archive bit is reset on each file

K. Process by which software and updates are distributed automatically to network computers

L. Target value used as a reference to determine if an activity or performance counter is out of expected tolerance

M. Switch between a primary and a redundant server that requires administrator or operator intervention

N. RAID 5 disk fault tolerant configuration using three or more hard disks and protecting against the failure of a single disk

O. Physically secure location for the storage of network hardware

P. Backup in which all data is backed up and the archive bit on each file is reset

Project 11.2	Backing Up and Restoring Data
Overview	Your best chance of recovering from a catastrophic system failure is to have a good backup of the data. A critical part of network management is to ensure that critical data is backed up on a regular basis. There will also be times when you need to run additional backups beyond your scheduled backups. For example, some applications and operating systems updates, including many service packs, recommend that you back up your data as the first step in the installation process.
	During this project you will simulate setting up backups for a network environment. You will configure a network share to act as the destination for network backups. You will back up selected files, configure regular backups, and restore data from a backup.

Outcomes	After completing this project, you will know how to: ▲ back up data to a network share ▲ configure periodic backups ▲ restore backup data
What you'll need	To complete this project, you will need: ▲ the worksheet below ▲ a computer running Windows XP ▲ a domain controller running Windows Server 2003
Completion time	45 minutes
Precautions	The instructions in this project assume you are working on a two-node network with one computer running Windows XP Professional and one computer running Windows Server 2003. If these computers are part of a larger classroom network, your instructor will provide you with alternate instructions. If working on an existing network, you must review the project steps with your network administrator. Your network administrator may need to make changes or additions to the instructions.

■ Part A: Prepare for backup

In this Part, you will prepare to test backup and restore operations. You will need a computer running Windows XP and a computer running Windows Server 2003. You should log on as an Administrator on both computers. Complete steps 1 through 7 on the computer running Windows XP and steps 8 through 15 on the computer running Windows Server 2003.

1. On the computer running Windows XP, open the **Start** menu and select **My Computer**.
2. Open the **C:** drive.
3. Under **File and Folder Tasks**, select **Make a new folder**.
4. Enter **BackupDest** as the folder name and press the Enter key.
5. Right-click **BackupDest** and select **Sharing and Security**.
6. Select **Share this folder**.
7. Click Permissions.
8. If not already set, check **Full Control** under **Allow**, as shown in Figure 11-1, and click OK.

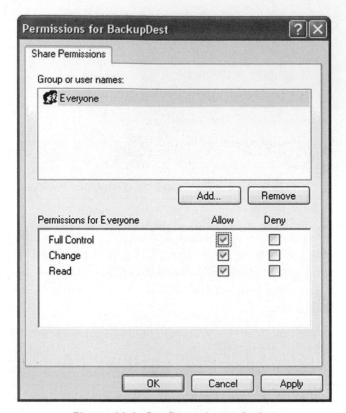

Figure 11-1: Configured permission

9. Click OK to create the share.

10. Open **BackupDest** and verify that the folder is empty. Exit **My Computer**.

11. On the computer running Windows Server 2003, open the **Start** menu and select **My Computer**.

12. Open the **C:** drive.

13. Right-click a clear area, and select **New** and then **Folder**. Name the folder **MySource**.

14. Open **MySource**.

15. Right-click the details pane, and select **New** and then **Text Document**. Name the file **Sample.txt**.

16. Double-click **Sample.txt** to launch **Notepad** with the file open.

17. Type the following: **This is a sample file for backup**.

18. Open the **File** menu and select **Save** and **Exit**.

    Note: Do not close **My Computer**.

■ Part B: Backup data

During this part of the project you will back up data to a shared network location. You will complete Part B on the computer running Windows Server 2003. You must have access to the network share on the computer running Windows XP.

1. Open the **Start** menu, point to **All Programs**, **Accessories**, and **Systems Tools**, and then select **Backup** to launch the **Backup** utility.

2. Click Next.

3. Leave **Back up files and setttings** (the default) selected, and click Next.

4. Select **Let me choose what to back up** and click Next.

5. Check **My Documents**. Expand **My Computer** and then drive **C:**, and check **MySource**.

6. Click Next.

7. Under **Choose a place to store my backup**, click Browse. If prompted that there is no removable drive, click OK to continue.

8. Double-click each time to navigate through **My Network Places**. Expand **Entire Network**, **Microsoft Windows Network**, **Busicorp**, and **the computer running Windows XP**, and select **BackupDest**, as shown in Figure 11-2.

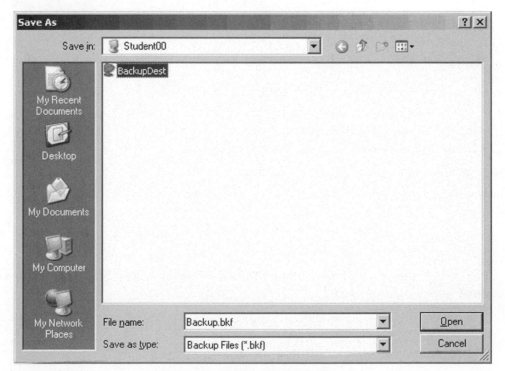

Figure 11-2: Backup destination

9. Click Open and then Save. The wizard should look like Figure 11-3.

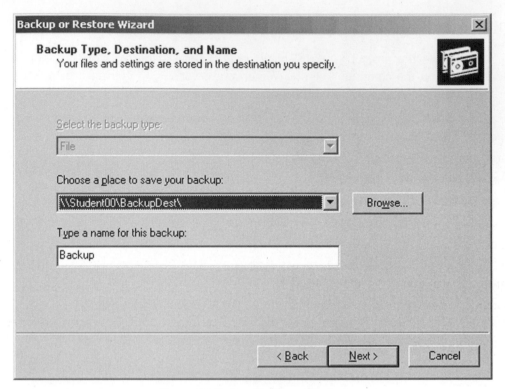

Figure 11-3: Destination selected

10. Click Next.

11. Review the advanced backup options. Click Advanced.

12. What kind of backup will run by default?

_____

13. Click Next to continue past the type of backup.

14. Select **Verify data after backup**. Why would you want to do this?

_____

15. Click Next.

16. You want to make sure a new backup file is created, so select **Replace the existing backups** and click Next.

17. When will the backup run by default?

_____

18. Click Next.

19. Review the summary. It should look like Figure 11-4.

Figure 11-4: Backup summary

20. Click Finish. A backup progress dialog box displays while the backup is running.

21. When the backup is complete, as shown in Figure 11-5, click Close.

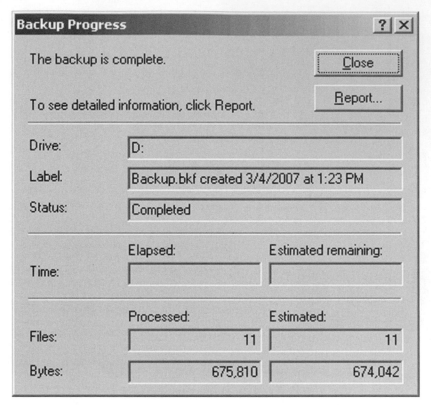

Figure 11-5: Completed backup

■ Part C: Restore data

During Part C you will restore from a backup and verify that the data is successfully restored. You will complete Part C on the computer running Windows Server 2003. You must have access to the network share on the computer running Windows XP.

1. In **My Computer**, click **Folders** on the toolbar to open the tree view pane on the left.
2. Expand **My Network Places**, **Entire Network**, **Microsoft Windows Network**, **Busicorp**, and **the computer running Windows XP**, and select **BackupDest**. What files, if any, do you see listed?

_____

3. Navigate to **C:\MySource**.
4. Right-click **Sample.txt** and select **Delete**.
5. When prompted to verify your action, click Yes.
6. Launch the **Backup** utility.
7. Click **Advanced Mode**, as indicated in Figure 11-6.

Figure 11-6: Choosing Advanced Mode

8. Select the **Restore and Manage Media** tab.

9. What information is provided in the backup identification label in the details pane?

_____

10. In the tree view pane on the left, expand **File** and then **Backup.bkf**, and then check the **C:** drive.

11. By default, what will happen if the file already exists?

_____

12. Click Start Restore.

13. When prompted to confirm restore, click OK. A **Restore** dialog box reports progress while the restore is running.

14. When the restore is complete, click Close.

15. In **My Computer**, check the contents of **MySource**. Was the file restored?

_____

16. Exit **My Computer**.

    Note: Do not exit the **Backup** utility.

■ Part D: Manage backups

During Part D you will configure a server to run periodic backups. You will complete Part D on a computer running Windows Server 2003.

1. In the **Backup** utility, select the **Schedule Jobs** tab.
2. Select the first Saturday that follows today's date and click Add Job. What happens?

_____

3. Click Next.
4. Leave **Back up everything on this computer** and click Next.
5. If not already set as the default, select ***computername*\\BackupDest** (replace *computername* with your Windows XP computer's name, **Student00** unless you used a different name) and click Next.
6. Leave the backup at default.
7. What is the default backup type?

_____

8. What would you choose if you wanted to back up changed files only and minimize the amount of time needed to run backups?

_____

9. Why?

_____

_____

10. What would you use if you wanted to back up changed files only and minimize the amount of time needed to restore data?

_____

11. Why is the time to restore minimized?

_____

_____

12. Click Next to continue to the **How to Back Up** page. Do not check **Verify data after backup** and click Next.
13. Choose to create a new backup file (replace the file) each time and click Next.
14. Enter **Weekly Full** in the **Job Name** field and click Set Schedule.
15. Under **Schedule Task**, choose **Weekly** from the drop-down list. Schedule the task to run every week at 12:00 A.M. Saturday. Your schedule should look like Figure 11-7.

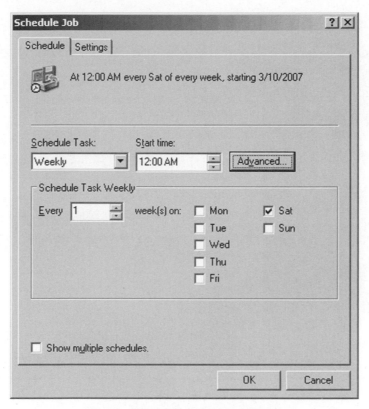

Figure 11-7: Completed schedule

16. Click OK.

17. When prompted for account information, leave the Administrator as the account under which to run the job. Enter the Administrator password (**P*ssword**, unless it has been changed) and click OK.

18. Click Next. If prompted for account information, enter the Administrator password and click OK.

19. The summary should look like the example shown in Figure 11-8. Review the summary and click Finish.

Figure 11-8: Backup summary

20. How has the schedule job calendar changed?

_____

21. Click one of the job icons. It should look like the example shown in Figure 11-9.

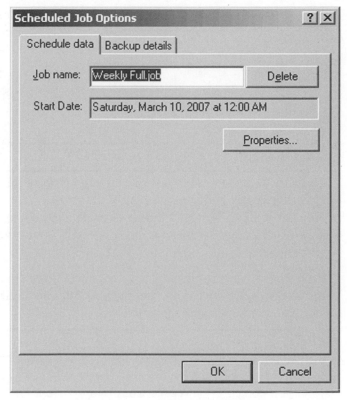

Figure 11-9: Scheduled job

22. Click OK to close the **Scheduled Job Options** dialog box.

23. Exit the **Backup** utility and close any open windows on the desktop.

Project 11.3	Monitoring Computer Activity
Overview	An important part of successful network management is careful monitoring. Different operating systems offer monitoring utilities and there are also several third-party products available.
	One flexible tool when using a Windows operating system is the Performance utility. It includes System Monitor, called Performance Monitor on older Windows versions. System Monitor lets you monitor real-time activity. The Performance utility also lets you log selected performance counters and sets alerts based on threshold values.
	You will work with System Monitor and some monitoring options during this project.
Outcomes	After completing this project, you will know how to:
	▲ monitor server activity
	▲ monitor a computer from a remote location

	▲ configure an alert
What you'll need	To complete this project, you will need: ▲ a computer running Windows Server 2003 ▲ a computer running Widows XP ▲ to have completed Project 11.2 ▲ this worksheet
Completion time	30 minutes
Precautions	The instructions in this project assume you are working on a two-node network with one computer running Windows XP Professional and one computer running Windows Server 2003. If these computers are part of a larger classroom network, your instructor will provide you with alternate instructions. If working on an existing network, you must review the project steps with your network administrator. Your network administrator may need to make changes or additions to the instructions.

During this project you will monitor computer activity using System Monitor. You will use one instance of System Monitor to monitor both a local server, the server on which it is running, and a remote computer. This lets you compare the results from two different computers. This is often used for side-by-side comparisons, but can also let you compare the effect of different activities on different network computers.

You will be using both computers during the project. You should be logged on as an Administrator on the computer running Windows Server 2003. At the beginning of this project, there should not be any user logged on at the computer running Windows XP.

■ Part A: Launch System Monitor

In Part A of the project, you will launch System Monitor and configure the performance counters you want to watch. You will generate activity on the computer running Windows Server 2003 to see the effect.

1. Open the **Start** menu, point to **Administrative Tools**, and select **Performance**. This launches the **Performance** utility with default performance counters selected in **System Monitor**, as shown in Figure 11-10.

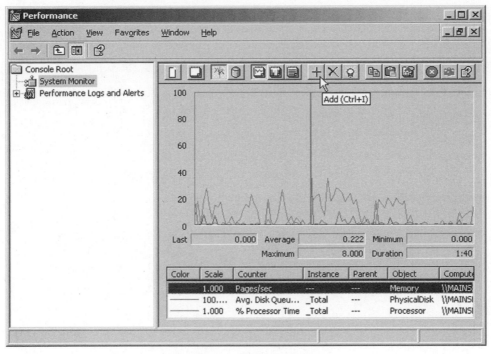

Figure 11-10: System Monitor

2. What are the default performance objects and counters?

_____

_____

_____

3. The **Add** toolbar button **(+)** is indicated in Figure 11-10. Click **Add**.

4. Select **Network Interface** as the performance object and **Bytes Total/sec** as the performance counter. Click Add and then Close.

5. Open the **Start** menu, point to **Administrative Tools**, and select **Active Directory Users and Computers**. Observe the performance counters as you open the utility. Exit the utility after it opens.

6. Open and then exit **Configure Your Server Wizard** from the **Administrative Tools**.

7. Launch **Network Monitor** from **Administrative Tools** and start a default capture. Leave the capture running.

8. What happens each time you launch a program?

_____

_____

■ Part B: Configure an alert

During Part B you will configure a performance alert based on a performance counter and threshold value. You will complete this part on the computer running Windows Server 2003.

1. In the **Performance** utility, expand **Performance Logs and Alerts** and select **Alerts**.
2. Right-click the details pane and select **New Alert settings**.
3. Name the alert **Processor Alert** and click OK.
4. Click Add.
5. Select **Processor** as the performance object, **%ProcessorTime** as the performance counter, and **Total** as the instance, as shown in Figure 11-11, and click Add and then Close.

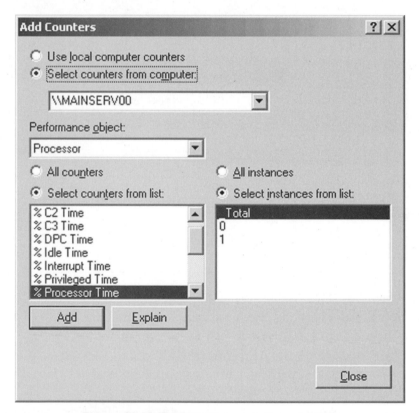

Figure 11-11: Performance counter selection

6. Set the threshold value as **Over a limit of 30** and sample every 1 second, as shown in Figure 11-12.

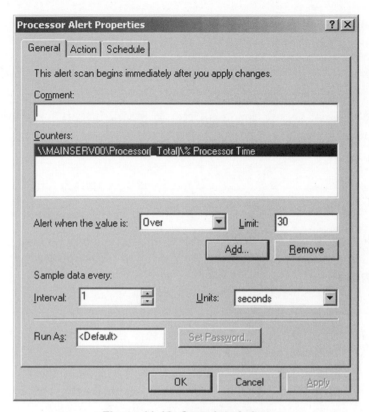

Figure 11-12: Completed alert

7. Select the **Action** tab.

8. Leave **Log an entry in the application event log** checked. Check **Send a network message to** and enter your current computer's name as the message destination.

9. Click OK to create the alert and start it, monitoring the computer.

10. Select **System Monitor**. What did System Monitor do while you were creating the alert?

_____

Note: Do not exit the **Performance** utility or **Network Monitor**.

■ Part C: Monitor a remote computer

You will add counters for the computer running Windows XP to System Monitor during Part C. You will observe the impact of activities that include both computers to compare the relative load on the computers.

During this part, if you receive a message at any time that the alert fired (triggered), clear the message and continue. Whether or not the alert triggers depends on your processor and processor speed.

1. In the **Performance** utility with **System Monitor** selected, click Add.

2. Type the name of the computer running Windows XP (**Student00**, unless you used an alternate name) under **Select counters from computer** and press the Enter key. What happens in the **System Monitor** window?

_____

3. Add the three original default counters (refer to Step 2 in Part A), but this time from the computer running Windows XP. Why don't you need to add Network Interface:Bytes Total/sec?

_____

_____

4. Click Close to close the **Add Counters** dialog box.

5. On the computer running Windows XP, log on as **Administrator**. What happens in **System Monitor**?

_____

6. In **Network Monitor**, select **Capture**, then **Stop**, then **Capture**, and then **Start**. When prompted to save the capture, click Yes.

7. Save the capture as **MyCap**. Save to the shared folder created on the Windows XP computer in Project 11.2 (BackupDest). What activity do you see **in System Monitor**?

_____

_____

8. Exit **Network Monitor**. Stop the capture when prompted. Do not save the capture when prompted.

9. Log off and then log on again to the computer running Windows XP. Which computer shows the most activity?

_____

10. Launch **My Computer** from the **Start** menu, expand **My Computer** so that the local drives are visible, and under **My Network Places**, locate and select the directory **BackupDest**.

11. Select all files in the directory, right-click, drag to drive **C:**, and release. When prompted, select **Move Here** to move the files. What is the effect on network activity?

_____

12. Select **Alerts**. Right-click your alert and run **Stop**. What is the advantage in doing this?

_____

13. Close **Performance**.

Project 11.4	Configuring Software Distribution
Overview	Automatic software distribution lets you install or remove software and software updates automatically. Possibly the most common use of automatic software distribution on current Windows computers is Automatic Updates—updates that can be downloaded from Microsoft Windows Update as program fixes, security enhancements, device driver updates, and so forth. When operating in a Windows Active Directory domain, you can use Group Policy to configure automatic software distribution to install and remove software. You can choose to configure distribution by user or by computer. During this project, you will configure Automatic Updates on a computer running Windows Server 2003. You will also configure automatic distribution for a user account.
Outcomes	After completing this project, you will know how to: ▲ configure Automatic Updates ▲ configure automatic software distribution
What you'll need	To complete this project, you will need: ▲ a domain controller running Windows Server 2003 ▲ a client computer running Windows XP Professional ▲ a Windows Server 2003 installation CD (or installation file set) ▲ this worksheet
Completion time	30 minutes
Precautions	The instructions in this project assume you are working on a two-node network with one computer running Windows XP Professional and one computer running Windows Server 2003. If the computer running Windows Server 2003 is part of a larger classroom network, your instructor will provide you with alternate instructions for configuring network and domain parameters. If working on an existing network, you must review the project steps with your network administrator. Your network administrator may need to make changes or additions to the instructions.

During this project, you will configure your domain controllers to download and install updates automatically from Windows Update. In a larger network, rather than having computers download updates individually, you might configure Microsoft Windows Server Update Services (WSUS). With WSUS, you can download the updates once to a local server and then use that server as the installation source for network clients. The method used here, configuring each client individually, is commonly used on small- to medium-sized networks.

You should be logged on to a computer running Windows Server 2003 at the beginning of this project.

■ Part A: Configure Automatic Updates

In Part A of this project, you will review information about and configure Automatic Updates on a computer.

1. Open the **Start** menu, and select **Control Panel** and then **Automatic Updates**.
2. Click the **How does Automatic Updates work?** link.
3. Expand and read **How are updates downloaded** and **How are updates installed** and answer the questions that follow:

   a. How does the Windows Update site know what updates to send you?

   _____

   _____

   b. What kind of information is *not* sent to Windows Update?

   _____

   _____

   c. What happens if you are disconnected from the Internet during the download process?

   _____

   _____

   d. What happens if the computer is turned off during a scheduled update?

   _____

   _____

   e. If an update requires restart, what is necessary to delay the restart?

   _____

   _____

4. Close the **Help** window.
5. Configure **Automatic Updates** to automatically download and install every date at 2:00 A.M. and then click OK.

6. What is the potential disadvantage of downloading and installing updates during normal working hours?

_____

_____

■ Part B: Configure software distribution

During Part B, you will configure software distribution on a computer running Windows Server 2003. You will need a Windows Server 2003 installation CD or the installation files to complete this part of the project.

1. Launch **My Computer**.
2. Create a folder at the root of the **C:** drive named **ForInstall**. Share the folder as **ForInstall**. You are sharing the folder so that it will be available to network clients.

    Note: Refer to Project 11.2 for instructions on how to create and share a folder, if necessary.
3. Navigate to the **\SUPPORT\TOOLS** folder on the installation CD and copy the folder contents to the **ForInstall** directory. This should include the files shown in Figure 11-13.

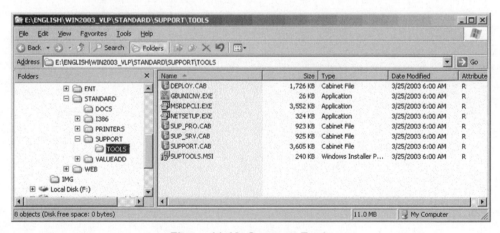

Figure 11-13: Support: Tools

4. Exit **My Computer**.
5. Launch **Active Directory Users and Computers** from **Administrative Tools**. If necessary, expand your domain.
6. Right-click **Busicorp.com**, and select **New** and then **Organizational Unit**. Name the OU **SoftwareTest** and click OK.
7. Right-click **SoftwareTest**, and select **New** and then **User**. Complete the user information, as shown in Figure 11-14, and click Next.

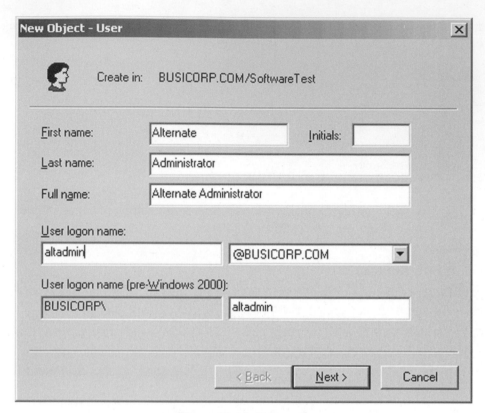

Figure 11-14: New user

8. Enter **P*ssword** in the **Password** and **Confirm password** prompts. Clear the check from **User must change password at next logon**, as shown in Figure 11-15, and click Next.

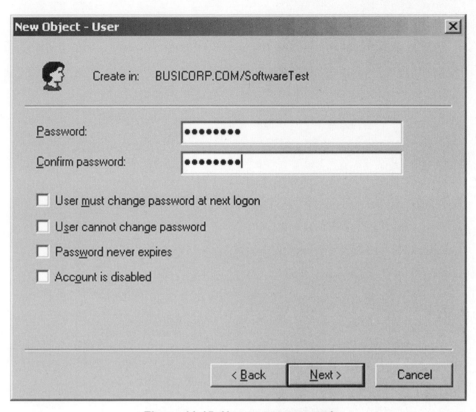

Figure 11-15: New user password

9. Click Finish.

10. Right-click **Alternate Administrator** and select **Properties**.

11. Select the **Member of** tab.

12. Click Add.

13. Enter **Administrators; Domain Admins** and click Check Names. Why should you click Check Names before continuing?

    Note: Domain Admins includes the Administrators group as a member. You are adding both for practice in adding multiple groups at the same time.

    _____

    _____

14. Click OK. The group list should look like Figure 11-16.

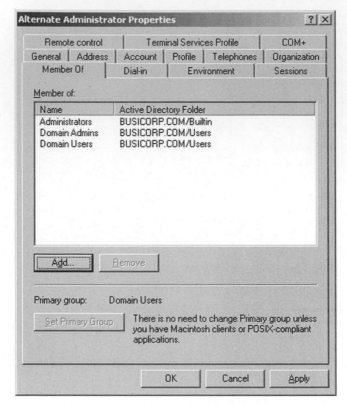

Figure 11-16: Group membership list

15. Click OK.

16. Right-click **SoftwareTest** and select **Properties**.

17. Select the **Group Policy** tab.

18. Click New and name the new **Group Policy Software Distribution**.

19. Click Edit.

20. Under **User Configuration**, expand **Software Settings** and select **Software Installation**.

21. Right-click **Software Installation**, and select **New** and then **Package**.

22. Browse under **My Network Places**, **Entire Network**, **Microsoft Windows Network**, **Busicorp**, your server (**MAINSERV00**, unless you used a different name), and select **ForInstall**.

23. Select **SUPTOOLS.MSI**, as shown in Figure 11-17, and click Open.

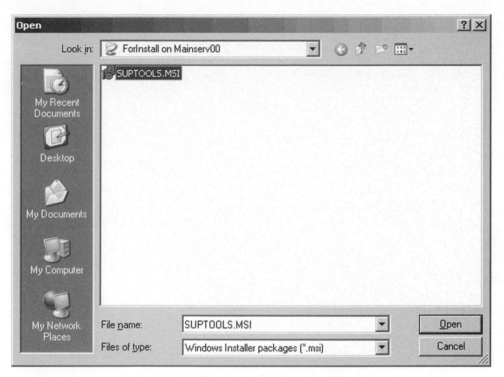

Figure 11-17: Selected software package

24. Leave the deployment method at the default selection **Published** and click OK. A detailed discussion of deployment options is beyond the scope of this project manual.

25. Software installation policy should look like the sample shown in Figure 11-18. Close the **Group Policy Editor**, click Close to close the **Properties** dialog box, and exit **Active Directory Users and Computers**.

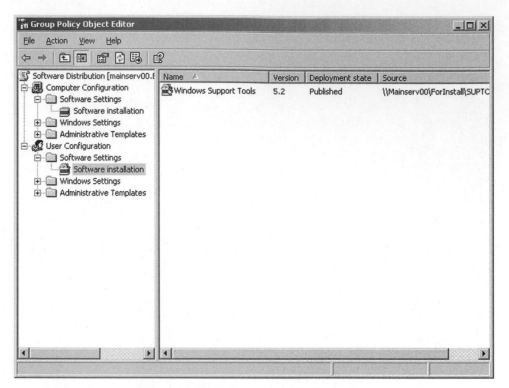

Figure 11-18: Software installation policy

26. Close any open windows on the computer.

■ Part C: Test software distribution

You will test software distribution during Part C. You will complete this part on a computer running Windows XP. If logged on as any user, log off before starting Part C.

1. Press CTRL + ALT + DEL to open the **Logon** dialog box.

2. Log on as **altadmin**, the user account you created in Part B of this project. There will be a short delay while the computer configures itself for the user.

3. Open the **Start** menu and point to **All Programs**. Notice the programs that are currently installed.

4. Select **Control Panel**, click **Add or Remove Programs**, and then click **Add New Programs**.

5. What do you see listed?

_____

_____

6. You will not be installing the software. You just want to check that it is available. Exit **Add or Remove Programs** and close the **Control Panel** window.

Project 11.5	Configuring SNMP Support
Overview	Network management systems are often used to make it easier for you to monitor, manage, and maintain enterprise networks. Management systems rely on SNMP and SNMP-compliant devices, which include computers running Windows operating systems. However, SNMP support is not installed by default because of possible security holes if it is not configured properly. An unauthorized management console could be used to collect system information, reconfigure computers, and even install hidden applications.
	During this project, you will install and configure SNMP support on your domain controller. You are simulating the procedures you would go through to set up for deploying a management system.
Outcomes	After completing this project, you will know how to: ▲ install SNMP support ▲ configure SNMP services
What you'll need	To complete this project, you will need: ▲ a running Windows Server 2003 ▲ Windows Server 2003 installation CD ▲ this worksheet
Completion time	15 minutes
Precautions	The instructions in this project assume you are working on a two-node network with one computer running Windows XP Professional and one computer running Windows Server 2003. If your domain controller is part of a larger classroom network, your instructor will provide you with alternate instructions.
	If working on an existing network, you must review the project steps with your network administrator. Your network administrator may need to make changes or additions to the instructions.

■ Part A: Install SNMP

In Part A, you will install SNMP, configure the SNMP service, and verify installation. You should be logged on to a computer running Windows Server 2003 as an Administrator.

1. Open the **Start** menu, and select **Control Panel** and then **Add or Remove Programs**.
2. Click **Add/Remove Windows Components**.
3. Select **Management and Monitoring Tools** and click Details.
4. Check **Simple Network Management Protocol** and **WMI SNMP Provider**, as shown in Figure 11-19, and click OK.

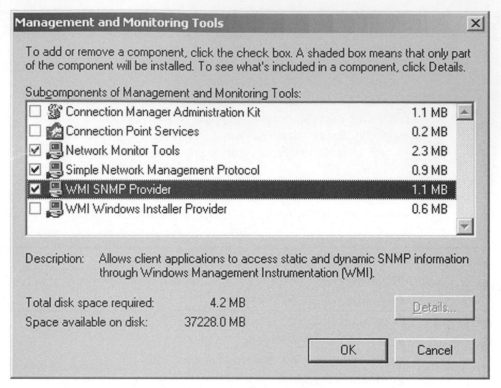

Figure 11-19: SNMP selections

5. Click Next. If prompted, insert the Windows Server 2003 installation CD.

6. When installation is complete, click Finish.

7. Exit **Add or Remove Programs**.

8. Open the **Start** menu, and select **Administrative Tools** and then **Services**.

9. Scroll down and locate **SNMP Service** and **SNMP Trap Service**. Verify that both services are running.

   Note: Do not exit the Services utility.

■ **Part B: Configure SNMP**

During Part B, you will configure SNMP parameters.

1. Select **SNMP Service**, right-click it, and select **Properties**. How is the start-up type configured?

_____

_____

2. Select the **Log on** tab. What account is configured as the **Log on** account?

_____

3. Select the **Agent** tab. Which types of services are identified as managed by this computer (checked)?

    Note: To view a description of what each service indicates, select that service and press F1.

    _____

4. Type your name in the **Contact** field.
5. Select the **Traps** tab. Enter **Default** in the **Community name** field and click Add to list.
6. Under **Trap destinations**, click Add. How can you specify a trap desitnation?

    _____

7. Click Cancel to close the **SNMP Service Configuration** dialog box.
8   Select the **Dependencies** tab. On what services, if any, does SNMP depend?

    _____

9. What services, if any, depend on SNMP?

    _____

10. Click OK to save the changes and close the properties.
11. Close **Services**.

12
NETWORK SECURITY

PROJECTS

Project 12.1	Understanding Key Concepts
Overview	Network security is a critical issue on any network. Networks are constantly under attack, from the Internet and other external sources as well as internally from network users. New types of attacks are continually being created. New viruses and other types of malicious software turn up daily. Understanding the terms and technologies related to security is an important part of security management. During this project, you will match various security-related terms to the definitions and descriptions of how they are used.
Outcomes	After completing this project, you will know how to: ▲ identify key terms and concepts related to network security
What you'll need	To complete this project, you will need: ▲ the worksheet below
Completion time	20 minutes
Precautions	None

The worksheet includes a list of security-related networking terms on the left and descriptions on the right. Match each term with the description that it most closely matches. You will *not* use all descriptions. Each description can be used only once.

____ DES

A. Attack that attempts to disrupt a network or its servers by flooding them with packets

____ RC4

B. Firewall filtering method that passes packets that match sessions initiated on the internal network

____ DoS

C. Term referring to any type of malicious software

____ Spyware

D. Situation where one failure is the direct cause of other failures

____ Trojan

E. 802.1x term referring to a client needing authentication

____ Worm

F. List of communication sessions between stations inside and outside the firewall that is maintained on the firewall

____ Malware

G. Self-propagating form of malicious software

___ Threat	H. Protected area of a network between the internal network and the Internet
___ Supplicant	I. Encryption standard used with WEP
___ Cascading failure	J. Process of sending packets with a fake source address
___ Certificate	K. Program that is expected to do one thing but actually does something else
___ DMZ	L. Term used to refer to the WAP during 802.1x authentication
___ Dynamic state list	M. Any potentially adverse occurrence that can harm the network or its data, interrupt network services, or cause a monetary loss
___ IP Spoofing	N. Secure identifier issued to a company, computer, or person that proves they are who they say they are
	O. Symmetric key encryption standard originally developed by IBM
	P. Software that monitors and records computer activity

Project 12.2	Using Auditing and Event Logs
Overview	You can configure auditing to automatically track selected network activities, even failed attempts to perform audited activities. Auditing can be set up individually on computers or, when configuring auditing for network computers on an Active Directory domain, through Group Policy.
	Audit events, as well as other types of events, are tracked in the Windows Event Logs. You should review the contents of the Event Logs on a periodic basis and whenever you have computer or network problems.
	During the project you'll set up auditing. You'll also review Event Log contents and save the contents of an Event Log to create a permanent record.
Outcomes	After completing this project, you will know how to: ▲ configure auditing

	▲ manage Event Logs
	▲ review Event Log contents
What you'll need	To complete this project, you will need:
	▲ the worksheet below
	▲ a computer running Windows XP
	▲ a domain controller running Windows Server 2003
Completion time	30 minutes
Precautions	The instructions in this project assume you are working on a two-node network with one computer running Windows XP Professional and one computer running Windows Server 2003. If these computers are part of a larger classroom network, your instructor will provide you with alternate instructions.
	If working on an existing network, you must review the project steps with your network administrator. Your network administrator may need to make changes or additions to the instructions.

■ Part A: Configure auditing policy

You configure auditing for your domain during Part A. You should be logged on to the computer running Windows Server 2003 as Administrator at the start of this project.

1. Open the **Start** menu, and select **Administrative Tools** and then **Active Directory Users and Computers**. If not already expanded, expand your domain.
2. Right-click the **Domain Controllers** container and select **Properties**.
3. Select the **Group Policy** tab. You should see the **Default Domain Controllers Policy** listed, as shown in Figure 12-1.

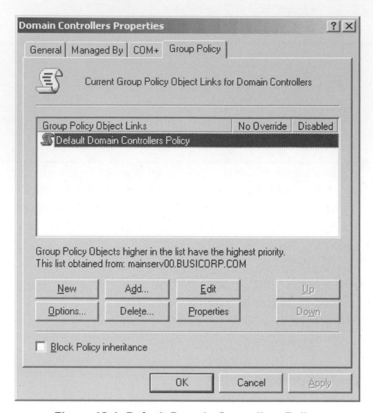

Figure 12-1: Default Domain Controllers Policy

4. Click Edit.

5. Under **Computer Configuration**, expand **Windows Settings**, **Security Settings**, and **Local Policy**. Select **Audit Policy**, as shown in Figure 12-2. Your policy settings may differ from those shown in the figure.

   Note: You can also open the **Security Settings** portion of **Default Domain Controllers Policy** by opening the **Start** menu, selecting **Administrative Tools** and then **Domain Controller Security Policy**. This gives you access to the **Security Settings** policies only.

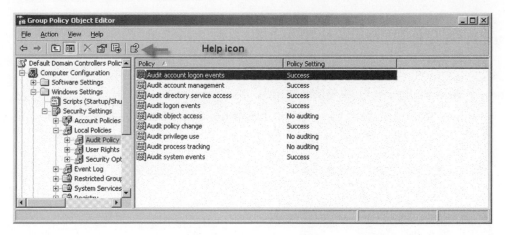

Figure 12-2: Audit Policy

6. Select **Audit logon events** and click the **Help** icon on the toolbar, as indicated in Figure 12-2.

7. Read the description. What is the advantage of logging failed attempts on a domain controller?

_____

8. What type of valid actions, those not related to a security breach, might generate the same?

_____

9. Take time to read the remaining audit policies in the Help window and answer the following questions:

    a. When would an Audit logon event be generated on domain controller?

_____

    b. What types of events are generated by the Audit system events policy?

_____

_____

10. Close **Help**.

11. Double-click **Audit account logon events**, enable the policy if not enabled, and check both **Success** and **Failure**. Click OK.

12. Double-click **Audit account management**, enable the policy if not enabled, and check both **Success** and **Failure**. Click OK.

13. Double-click **Audit policy change**, enable the policy if not enabled, and check both **Success** and **Failure**. Click OK.

14. Double-click **Audit system events**, enable the policy if not enabled, and check both Success and Failure. Click OK.

    Note: Do not close **Group Policy Object Editor**.

■ **Part B: Configure security policies for audit logs**

In Part B, you will view and modify policies that affect security logs.

1. Under **Local Policies**, click **User Rights Assignment**.
2. Scroll down, locate, and select **Manage auditing and security logs**, as shown in Figure 12-3.

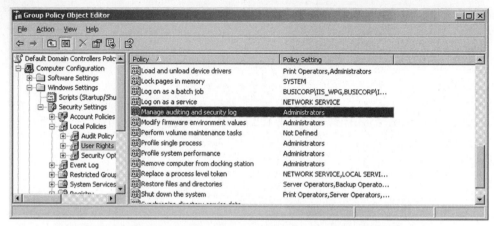

Figure 12-3: Manage auditing and security logs rights assignment

3. Double-click to open the policy. What users have the right to manage auditing and security logs?

_____

_____

4. What is the potential risk of granting this right to other users or groups?

_____

_____

5. Under **Local Policies**, click **Security Options**.
6. Locate and select **Audit: Shut down system immediately if unable to log security audits**, as shown in Figure 12-4.

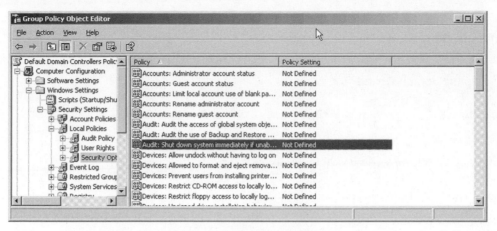

Figure 12-4: Security Options

7. What is the potential risk of enabling this policy?

_____

_____

8. Double-click and enable the policy, and then click OK.
9. Select **Event Log**, as shown in Figure 12-5.

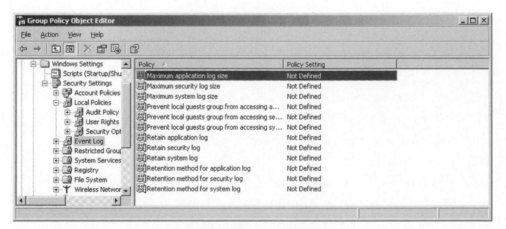

Figure 12-5: Event Log policies

10. Select **Maximum security log size** and click the **Help** icon. What is the default log size on your domain controller?

_____

_____

11. In the **Help** window, select and review **Retain security log** and **Retention method for security log**.

12. Close the **Help** window.
13. Double-click **Retain security log** and check **Define this policy setting**.
14. What is the default period?

_____

15. Click OK.
16. What policy setting will be enabled automatically?

_____

17. Click OK.
18. What is the potential risk if you don't archive the security log every week?

_____

19. Close **Group Policy Object Editor** and then click OK to close the **Domain Controller Policies**.
20. Exit **Active Directory Users and Computers**.

■ Part C: Generate and view events

In Part C, you will generate Account Logon events and view them in Event Viewer. You will use your domain controller.

1. Log off your domain controller.
2. Press Ctrl + Alt + Del to display the logon dialog.
3. Enter the password for Administrator incorrectly and click OK.
4. Click OK to clear the warning.
5. Enter the password for Administrator correctly and click OK.
6. Open the **Start** menu, and select **Administrative Tools** and then **Event Viewer**.
7. Select **Security**. You should see entries similar to those shown in Figure 12-6.

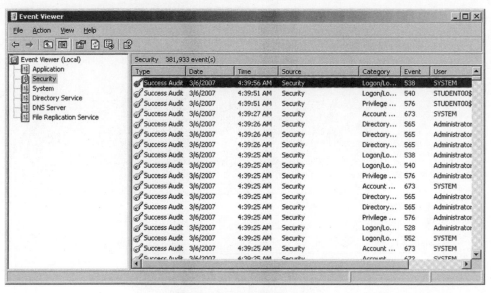

Figure 12-6: Security log

8. Locate and double-click the most recent **Failure Audit** event. What does it tell you?

    _____

9. What is given as the client address?

    _____

10. What does this tell you and why?

    _____

    _____

11. Click Cancel.

12. Launch **Active Directory Users and Computers**.

13. Position the windows so you can see both **Event Viewer** and **Active Directory Users and Computers**.

14. Right-click **Users** and choose **New User**.

15. Fill in the dialog box, as shown in Figure 12-7, and then click Next.

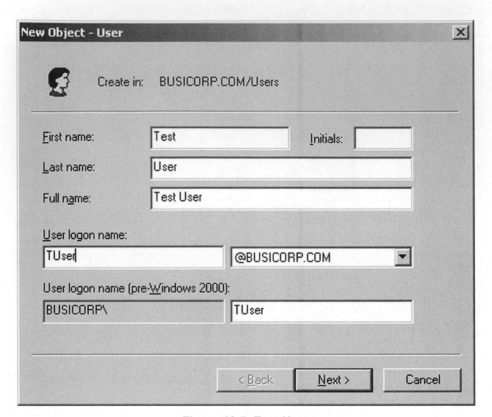

Figure 12-7: Test User

16. Enter and confirm **P*ssword** as the password and click Next.

17. Click Finish.

18. In the **Event Viewer** window, right-click **Security** and choose **Refresh**.

19. Double-click the bottom **Account Management** event (the first **Account Management** event after the events generated by the Administrator logon), as shown in Figure 12-8.

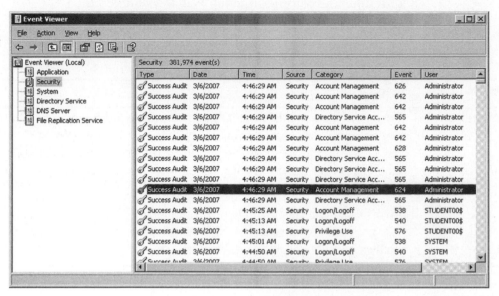

Figure 12-8: Account management events

20. Double-click the event. What does it tell you?

_____

21. Click the Up arrow until you get to the next **Account Management** event. What does this event tell you?

_____

22. Click the Up arrow and review through the remaining **Account Management** events.
23. After reviewing the events, click Cancel.
24. Close **Active Directory Users and Computers** and **Event Viewer**.

Project 12.3	Managing Account Lockout Policy
Overview	Account lockout policy is one of the best tools available for preventing unauthorized access attempts. You can set the number of attempts before the account is locked, the time-out period before account locking resets itself, and for how long the account remains locked. During this project you will configure and test account lockout policy for your domain.
Outcomes	After completing this project, you will know how to: ▲ configure account lockout policy ▲ test account lockout policy
What you'll need	To complete this project, you will need:

	▲ a domain controller running Windows Server 2003
	▲ a computer running Windows XP
	▲ to complete Project 12.2
	▲ this worksheet
Completion time	30 minutes
Precautions	The instructions in this project assume you are working on a two-node network with one computer running Windows XP Professional and one computer running Windows Server 2003. If these computers are part of a larger classroom network, your instructor will provide you with alternate instructions.
	If working on an existing network, you must review the project steps with your network administrator. Your network administrator may need to make changes or additions to the instructions.

■ Part A: Configure account lockout policy

In this part of the project, you will configure account lockout policy for the domain. You should be logged on to your domain controller as Administrator.

1. Launch **Active Directory Users and Computers** and display the properties for your domain.

2. Select the **Group Policy** tab. You should see **Default Domain Policy** listed, as in Figure 12-9.

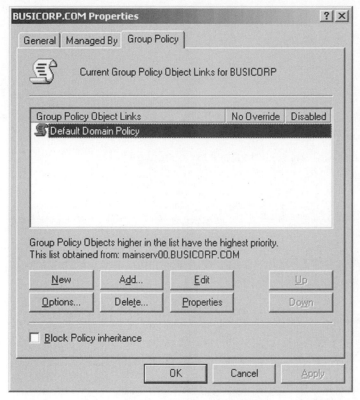

Figure 12-9: Default Domain Policy

3. Click Edit.

4. Under **Computer Configuration**, expand **Windows Settings**, **Security Settings**, and **Account Policies**. Select **Account Lockout**, as in Figure 12-10.

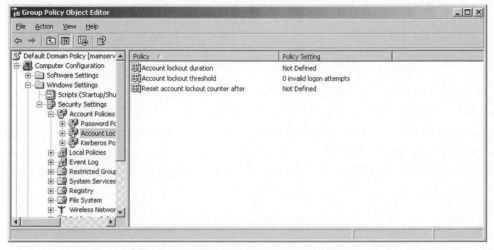

Figure 12-10: Account Lockout policies

5. How is account lockout currently configured?

_____

_____

6. Double-click **Account lockout duration**. Click **Define this policy setting** and set the lockout duration 10 minutes.

7. Click OK. What other suggested values are displayed?

_____

_____

8. Click OK.

9. Double-click **Account lockout threshold** and change the value to **2**, and then click OK. Your policy settings should look like Figure 12-11.

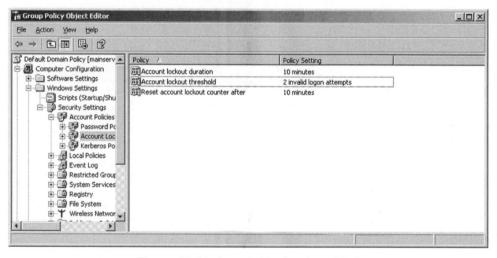

Figure 12-11: Account lockout enabled

10. Close the **Group Policy Object Editor**, click OK to close the domain **Properties** dialog box, and exit **Active Directory User and Computers**.

11. Launch **Event Viewer** and select the **Security** log. You are going to clear the log to make it easier to see entries generated by account lockout.

12. Select **Action** and then **Clear all events**. Click No when prompted to save the log contents.

13. What does the event that was entered tell you?

_____

Note: Do not exit **Event Viewer**.

■ Part B: Test account lockout policy

You will lock a user account and generate lockout events in Part B. Shut down and restart the computer running Windows XP before starting this part of the project.

1. Attempt to log on as **TUser**. Enter the wrong password. What does the dialog box tell you?

    _____

2. Click OK and attempt to log on again as **TUser** with the wrong password. What happens?

    _____

3. Click OK and attempt to log on again as **TUser** with the wrong password. What happens?

    _____

4. Click OK and attempt to log on again as **TUser** with the correct password. What happens?

    _____

5. Click OK to clear the dialog box.

■ Part C: Unlock the account and cover your tracks

During Part C, you will unlock the user account and take actions to cover your tracks.

1. In **Event Viewer**, right-click **Security** and select **Refresh**.
2. Locate and open the first (bottommost) failure audit event. It should look similar to the example shown in Figure 12-12.

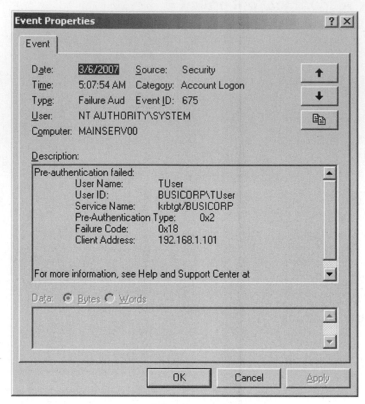

Figure 12-12: Failure audit event

3. What does this event tell you?

    _____

4. Click the Up arrow. What does the next event tell you?

    _____

5. Click the Up arrow until you locate the event showing the account locked out, like the example shown in Figure 12-13.

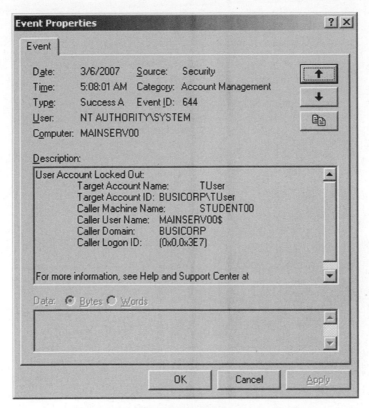

Figure 12-13: Account locked out event

6. Is this a success event instead of a failed event?

_____

7. Click Cancel.

8   Launch **Active Directory Users and Computer**. Select the **Users** container and locate **Test User**.

9. Right-click **Test User** and select **Properties**.

10. Select the **Account** tab. Notice that the account is locked, as shown in Figure 12-14.

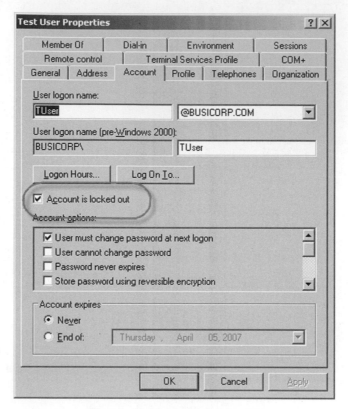

Figure 12-14: Locked account

11. Uncheck **Account is locked out** and then click OK.

12. Exit **Active Directory Users and Computers**.

13. Refresh the **Security** log. Should the events generated when you unlocked the account be Success or Failed Audit events, and why?

_____

14. Open the most recent event. It should show that the account was unlocked. If not, click the Down arrow until you locate the account unlock events.

15. Using the procedures described earlier, clear the **Security** log. What events are now in the log?

_____

16. What would another administrator be able to tell about the attempted security breach that just occurred?

_____

17. What might cause an administrator to think that someone has just tried to clear his or her tracks?

_____

_____

18. Exit **Event Viewer**.

Project 12.4	Managing Password Policy
Overview	User accounts and passwords are part of your first line of defense against unauthorized access. Each user should have his or her own user account. Each user account should be protected by a password, and passwords should be changed on a periodic basis.
	One potential problem is that many users tend to select weak, or easily guessed, passwords. You can use password policies to control password length, complexity, and how often users must change passwords.
	During this project, you will configure and test password policies. You will set domain policies that apply to all domain user accounts.
Outcomes	After completing this project, you will know how to:
	▲ configure password policy
	▲ test password policy
What you'll need	To complete this project, you will need:
	▲ a domain controller running Windows Server 2003
	▲ a Windows XP Professional domain member
	▲ a domain user account
	▲ to complete Project 12.2
	▲ this worksheet
Completion time	30 minutes
Precautions	The instructions in this project assume you are working on a two-node network with one computer running Windows XP Professional and one computer running Windows Server 2003. If these computers are part of a larger classroom network, your instructor will provide you with alternate instructions.
	If working on an existing network, you must review the project steps with your network administrator. Your network administrator may need to make changes or additions to the instructions.

■ Part A: Configure password policy

In Part A, you will configure the default domain policy to set password policy. The password policy, unless it has been changed, is at the Active Directory domain default settings.

1. Launch **Active Directory User and Computers** and display the **Busicorp.com** domain properties.

2. Select the **Group Policy** tab, verify that **Default Domain Policy** is selected, and click Edit.

3. Under **Computer Configuration**, expand **Windows Settings**, **Security Settings**, and **Account Policies**. Select **Password Policy**, as in Figure 12-15.

4. Default password policies are shown in Figure 12-15. Your settings should be similar.

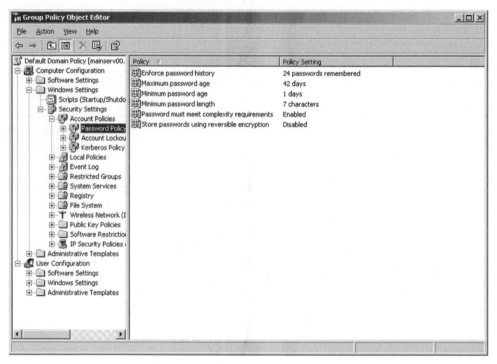

Figure 12-15: Domain password policy

5. Select **Enforce password history** and click the **Help** icon. Review each of the password policies and then close the **Help** window.

   a. What is the possible risk in setting the maximum password age policy to too great a value?

   _____

   _____

   _____

b. What is the possible risk in setting the minimum password length too long?

_____

_____

_____

c. What is the impact, if any, on existing passwords when you change password length or complexity so that they are no longer valid?

_____

_____

_____

d. What is the maximum value for Enforce password history?

_____

_____

_____

6. Open **Maximum password age**, increase the value to **60**, and click OK.

7. Open **Minimum password length**, increase the value to **8**, and click OK. Your password policies should look like Figure 12-16.

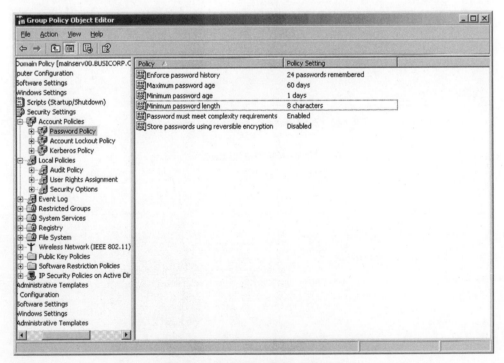

Figure 12-16: Modified policies

8. Close the **Group Policy Object Editor**, and then click OK to close the domain **Properties** dialog box.

   Note: Do not exit **Active Directory User and Computers**.

■ Part B: Test password policy

In Part B, you will test which password policies apply when an administrator resets a user's password.

1. Select the **Users** container and locate **Test User**.
2. Right-click **Test User**, and select **Reset Password** to open the **Reset Password** dialog box, as shown in Figure 12-17.

Figure 12-17: Reset Password dialog box

3. Enter and confirm the password **Password** and click OK.
4. What happens?

_____

5. Click OK.
6. Test the following passwords:

   P*ssword   One234&5
   P@$$WORD   1@#rr
   tHisIzMin2   ne234567
   One234%

7. Which passwords are accepted as valid?

_____

_____

_____

_____

8. For the remaining passwords, explain why they were not accepted.

_____

_____

_____

_____

9. Set the password to **P*ssword**.

10. Check **User must change password at next logon** (see Figure 12-18) and click OK.

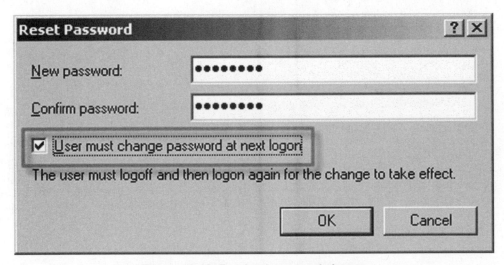

Figure 12-18: Forcing password change

11. What is the advantage to checking **User must change password at next logon** when resetting a user's password?

_____

_____

12. Which password policies are not enforced when an administrator resets a user's password and how do you know this?

_____

_____

_____

13. Exit **Active Directory Users and Computers**.

■ Part C: Test passwords

In Part C, you will test which password policies apply when a user makes password changes. You will complete this part of the project on the computer running Windows XP. If logged on to the computer, log off.

1. Press CTRL + ALT + DEL to open the **Log On to Windows** dialog box shown in Figure 12-19.

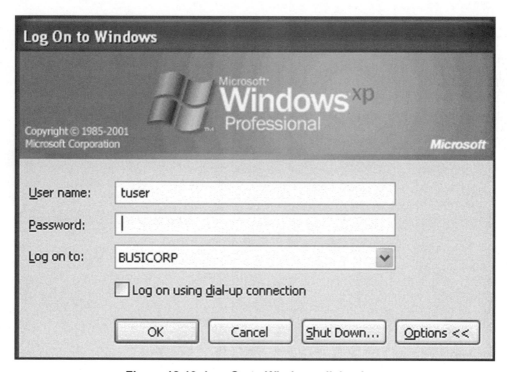

Figure 12-19: Log On to Windows dialog box

2. Log on using the password **P*ssword**. What happens?

_____

3. Why?

_____

4. Click OK.
5. Enter **password** as the new password and click OK.
6. What happens?

_____

7. How does this password violate password policy?

_____

8. Click OK to close the warning. Enter the old password (**P*ssword**) and then **P*ssword** as the new password and click OK.

9. What happens?

_____

10. How does this password violate password policy?

_____

11. Click OK to close the warning. Enter the old password (**P*ssword**) and **P@$$word** as the new password and click OK.

12. What happens?

_____

13. Click OK.

14. After logon is complete, press CTRL + ALT + DEL to open the **Windows Security** dialog box.

15. Click Change Password.

16. Enter the old password and **passW@4d** as the new password (see Figure 12-20), and then click OK.

Figure 12-20: Change Password dialog box

17. What happens?

_____

18. How does this password violate password policy?

_____

19. Click Cancel and then click Cancel.

20. The dialog box displayed for any password change error is shown in Figure 12-21.

Figure 12-21: Password complexity error

21. What is the advantage to displaying the same dialog box, no matter what error is preventing the user from changing the password?

_____

22. What option does Test User have for changing the user account password?

_____

Project 12.5	Designing for Security
Overview	An important part of securing your network is being aware of potential security problems and designing your network to be secure. This includes hardening the network as a whole, as well as individual clients and servers on the network.
	The Internet has hundreds of sources of security information and security tools. Operating system and application manufacturers have information available online for their specific products. Other sources, such as SearchSecurity.com, provide links to information and security tools. However, it is important to exercise caution and download from known source only. Some "security" websites are actually distribution points for viruses, Trojans, and other types of attacks.
	During this project, you will answer questions related to network security design and securing network computers.
Outcomes	After completing this project, you will know how to: ▲ recognize security threats ▲ design a network to minimize threats ▲ configure computers to minimize threats

What you'll need	To complete this project, you will need: ▲ this worksheet
Completion time	30 minutes
Precautions	None

■ Part A: Secure network design

In Part A, you will make network design decisions based on security requirements. Some of the questions refer to the network diagram shown in Figure 12-22.

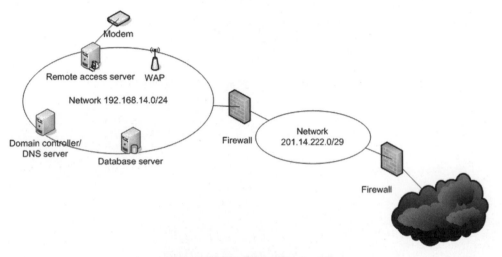

Figure 12-22: Sample network

1. What kind of network is network 201.14.222.0/29?

    _____

2. What types of servers would you place on that network?

    _____

3. You are using an inner firewall that implements dynamic packet filtering. How does that impact the data passed by the firewall?

    _____

    _____

4. What would be necessary to configure the network using a single firewall?

    _____

    _____

5. What are the possible entry points into the network?

   _____

   _____

6. Which is likely the biggest security risk and why?

   _____

   _____

7. The WAP supports both WEP and WPA. Which is more secure?

   _____

8. What authentication protocol does WPA use?

   _____

9. What configuration changes should you make in relation to the WAP's SSID?

   _____

   _____

10. What can you use to have the web server identify itself and your company to visitors?

   _____

   _____

11. The network is configured as a Windows Active Directory domain. Remote users are authenticated by the domain. You suspect that domain user names have been compromised. What policies can you implement to help detect and prevent unauthorized access and how would they help?

   _____

   _____

   _____

   _____

   _____

12. The network is attacked by a flood of SYN packets. What is the general term for this type of attack?

   _____

13. What is the difference between a DoS and a DDoS attack?

   _____

   _____

14. You want to add a subnetwork as a screened subnet. What would this require?

_____

_____

■ Part B: Network server placement

In Part B, you will place network servers on a network diagram. You will use Figure 12-23 with this part of the project.

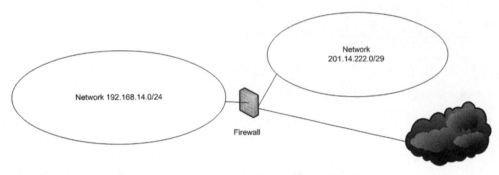

Figure 12-23: Another sample network

Indicate on Figure 12-23 where you would place the following:

- Public web server
- Private web server
- E-mail relay server
- Database server
- Domain controller/DNS server
- NAT Proxy server

■ Part C: Secure network computers

You will make security decisions that relate to individual network computers in Part C.

1. What steps can you take to prevent virus infection?

_____

_____

_____

_____

_____

2. What is the advantage of implementing a software-based firewall on each client computer?

   _____

3. You want to ensure that the same password policy is used for all computers in an Active Directory domain. Where should the group policy object be linked?

   _____

4. What is the potential risk if spyware is installed on a client computer?

   _____

   _____

5. What can a rootkit do if installed on a computer?

   _____

6. How is a worm propagated between computers?

   _____

   _____

7. How does a spam filter protect a computer?

   _____